HAY &
STARDUST

Also by Ruth Burgess:

At Ground Level (out of print)
Praying for the Dawn (with Kathy Galloway)
A Book of Blessings
Friends and Enemies
Eggs and Ashes (with Chris Polhill)
Hear My Cry
Candles & Conifers

HAY & STARDUST

Resources for Christmas to Candlemas

Ruth Burgess

WILD GOOSE PUBLICATIONS

Contents of book © the individual contributors
Compilation © 2005 Ruth Burgess

First published 2005, reprinted 2007

Wild Goose Publications, 4th Floor, Savoy House, 140 Sauchiehall St, Glasgow G2 3DH, UK.
Wild Goose Publications is the publishing division of the Iona Community.
Scottish Charity No. SCO03794. Limited Company Reg. No. SCO96243.
www.ionabooks.com

ISBN 978-1-905010-00-4

Cover painting and internal illustration © Scott Riley

**The publishers gratefully acknowledge the support of the Drummond Trust,
3 Pitt Terrace, Stirling FK8 2EY in producing this book.**

A catalogue record for this book is available from the British Library.

Overseas distribution:
Australia: Willow Connection Pty Ltd, Unit 4A, 3-9 Kenneth Road, Manly Vale, NSW 2093
New Zealand: Pleroma, Higginson Street, Otane 4170, Central Hawkes Bay
Canada: Novalis/Bayard Publishing & Distribution, 10 Lower Spadina Ave.,
Suite 400, Toronto, Ontario M5V 2Z2

Permission to reproduce any part of this work in Australia or New Zealand should be sought
from Willow Connection.

Printed by Bell & Bain, Thornliebank, Glasgow

GENERAL CONTENTS

CONTENTS IN DETAIL

Key to symbols	
✝	Prayer
✝	Reading
✛	Biblical reflection
☙	Liturgy
((◎))	Responses
♫	Song
☙	Story
🎭	Drama

Key to symbols	
✝	Prayer
𝒢	Reading
✣	Biblical reflection
𝄞	Liturgy
((◎))	Responses
♫	Song
🕮	Story
🎭	Drama

Key to symbols	
✟	Prayer
𝄞	Reading
✣	Biblical reflection
𝄡	Liturgy
(((O)))	Responses
♫	Song
🐌	Story
🎭	Drama

*For Frances
and for Ali;
sharers of snowdrops,
lighters of candles,
travellers of life*

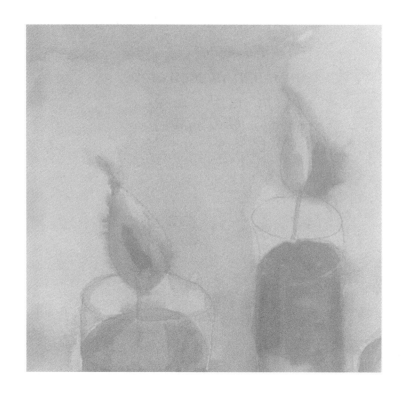

INTRODUCTION

Hay & Stardust is a resource book which covers the period from Christmas Day to Candlemas. It is a companion volume to *Candles & Conifers* (Wild Goose Publications), which covers the period from All Saints' Day to Christmas Eve.

Whilst a number of complete liturgies are included, most of the material in this book consists of the stuff that liturgies are made of – stories, prayers, ceremonies, songs, responses, poems and biblical reflections.

Also included are a number of Christmas plays; props include puppets, knuckle-dusters, big flashes, sticking plasters, sacks and stars! You have been warned.

The material in *Hay & Stardust* is arranged chronologically, with sections relating to particular days and to general Christmastide themes. I have, in the contents pages, classified the material into types, for ease of reference.

My grateful thanks to all the contributors for their rich and imaginative material that I have been privileged to edit. One book swiftly turned into two! Opening my mail has been a delight.

Thanks are also due to the Wild Goose Publications team, to Jane Darroch-Riley, Alex O'Neill, Tri Boi Ta and Sandra Kramer for their professionalism, encouragement and support; and to Neil Paynter, whose attention to detail is becoming legendary; I am hugely and gratefully in debt.

One of our regular contributors, Ian Cowie, died whilst this book was being put together. He and his prayers and his humour will be greatly missed. I close with words from his New Year Blessing:

Now we arise and go forth on the journey before us,
knowing that, where Christ leads, life is a journey home.
Therefore we travel in faith, in hope and in love.

Ruth Burgess
Summer 2005

CHRISTMAS DAY

AT HALF PAST THREE IN THE MORNING

On Christmas day at half past three in the morning I woke up and I saw light coming out of my window. I thought it was light, but it wasn't light, it was just a lamppost making shadows. So I started to open my presents, and when I was on the second one before the last my daddy came in and said: 'Put the presents down and try and get back to sleep.'

Graham, aged 7

WHO IS WITHOUT, WHO IS WITHIN?

Cold dark nights, warm bright lights;
Christmas is the hardest and the kindest time.
Memories and expectations, confrontations, salutations!

Who is without, who is within?
A question still at Bethlehem's inn.

What awaits the Christ child now
is in our power to decide,
as the world attends another Christmastide.

Liz Gregory-Smith

Written the year that Palestinian Christians and Muslims took refuge in the Church of the Nativity in Bethlehem.

TABGHA

Jesus,
You had a birthday today.
A little boy stood,
and solemnly set alight
every stub of candle
that he could dig out of the sand tray
at the front of the church.

And growing in the stillness,
gloriously reflected
in your golden halo
and in his dark eyes,
there was light, dancing.

Ruth Burgess

Note: Tabgha is the location of a church near Lake Galilee.

IN YOUR ARMS I LIE

In your arms
I lie –

Full-filled,
stilled

Complete-replete,
dribbling milk.

Beryl Jeanne

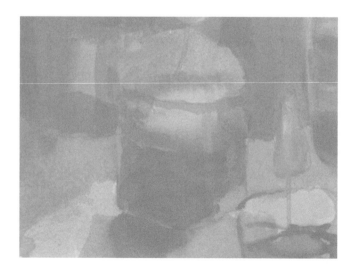

PRAISE GOD

Praise God!

Praise God
for the joy and delight of children
and grandchildren.

Praise God
for the calmness after the storm
of shrieks and wrapping being shredded.

Praise God
for laughter,
for thank you's,
for words of wonder and surprise.

Praise God
for Bethlehem's birth,
for Calvary's suffering,
for Easter's life.

Praise God!

Thom M Shuman

CHRISTMAS RESPONSES

A child is born
A child to save us
WE SHARE THE NEWS WITH GREAT JOY

A child is born
A child to challenge us
WE SHARE THE NEWS WITH GREAT JOY

A child is born
A child for the world
WE SHARE THE NEWS WITH GREAT JOY

Ruth Burgess

WE REMEMBER YOUR PROMISES

Here we are, Lord;
we are not many,
nor are we very wise
or powerful,
nor rich by the standards of the world,
but we do come
joyful and triumphant
on this special day,
because of what you have done.

On this day
we remember your promises
that you will never leave us
nor forsake us,
that you would show your love for us in a very special way,
that you would always let us know that you love us,
despite all our fears.

On this day
we joyfully remember you
creeping in very quietly
and very vulnerably
among us
in Jesus Christ, born of Mary.
Born to be with us,
born to love us,
born to save us,
born to free us.

Please forgive us
for forgetting all this so often;
for thinking of you in human terms –
for imagining you to be a fearsome
far-off sort of God,
angry and vengeful;
or thinking of you as a petulant parent,
rewarding us with sweets when we are good
and smacking us when we are bad.
Forgive us for blaming you when things go wrong

and ignoring you when we think we are in control;
for being so busy and caught up in our own concerns
that we don't even take time
to stop and listen to yours.

Help us
to come to your birthplace
and to your birthday.
Help us to let you enter our lives.
Speak your word of power in our hearts
and change us, once again.

John Harvey

LOVE AND DANGER

Christmas Day:
angels and stars,
shepherds and travellers,
a new born child.

An old story
full of love and danger,
laying bare the beauty
of an amazing God.

Ruth Burgess

HOW OLD WERE THE ANGELS?

Luke 2:25–38

How old were the angels?

About five years old,
appearing on stage,
blinking in the bright lights
with a tinsel halo askew.

But how old were those
in the Gospel story the children were telling,
the angels that appeared
to Mary, and then to Joseph and then
to the shepherds in the fields?

As old as the hills, and as here-and-now
as human hopes and fears.
What's more, those angels were frightening,
warriors with flaming swords,
not mixed infants with mums looking on:
that's why their first words were 'Do not be afraid'.

But how old were they?

Who can tell? Angels exist in God's time,
not according to our clocks and calendars.
They see eternity in the blink of an eye.

More to the point, how old
were hands that held the newborn child,
faces on which those wide-open eyes focused,
voices which gave a blessing?
Simeon and Anna were rich in years,
who had waited so long to see their Lord,
who sang his praises and announced salvation.

How old were these angels?
About the age of many who sit in our pews:
as old as wisdom, as young as hope.

Jan Sutch Pickard

ONCE IN BETHLEHEM

ON THE MOUNTAINSIDE

Words and music: Pat Livingstone

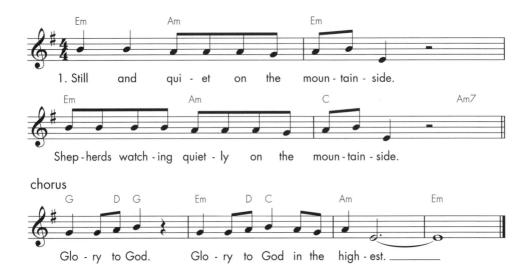

chorus

Sheep asleep on the mountainside.
Angels started singing on the mountainside.

Chorus

No more quiet on the mountainside.
Many, many angels on the mountainside.

Chorus

Bright white light on the mountainside.
Shining, lighting, flooding all the mountainside.

Chorus

Scared, afraid on the mountainside.
Shepherds shouting, running on the mountainside.

Pat Livingstone

SHEPHERD

Until tonight
I could not fit the size of God
into my head.
I thought he was a God
for prophets and kings,
men of words and wisdom.
But tonight I am looking at God made small,
small enough for me,
small enough to pick up
and hold like a lamb.
I could not talk to a God in the clouds;
but tonight when I look and smile
and talk nonsense to this
tiny thing, I know that I am
talking to God.
And it is God who smiles
back at me and waves his
perfect hands in delight.
And tonight in your smallness, God,
you seem bigger and more powerful
to me than you ever did before.
I can hold you now,
hold you in my head
and hold you in my arms,
and know that you are holding me in yours.

Lisa Debney

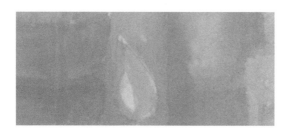

MARY

Your eyes are open now.
Those eyes which will open
the eyes of others.
You study my face
and, just for the moment,
though you came for the world,
you are mine and mine alone.
I made you and you made me
and we gaze at each other
in equal wonderment.

Your eyes are open now, and so dark-bright –
sent from a night
full of light and stars –
that I could watch you for ever,
watch your chest rise and fall
as you breathe the cattle-soaked air.
I would like this moment to last for ever,
you are so wonderful to me,
so truly wonderful as you are.

But not my will, Lord,
but yours be done.
I must hand you over
for the world cries out for you,
though I cry out to let you go.
Just for tonight
let the future
leave us in peace.
Close your eyes, baby.
Close your bright eyes
on the dusty darkness
of the world.
There is majesty in you
but for now let it hide,
let it hide like a gem
while you sleep.

Lisa Debney

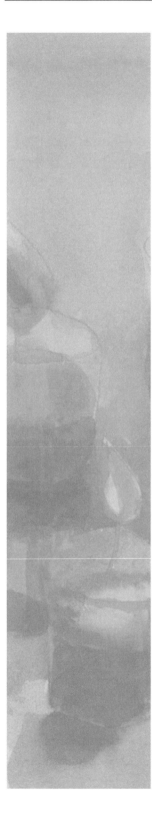

JOSEPH

Here I stand,
holding the tiny, warm weight
of God in my hands.
Such a tiny weight
to lift the huge weight
of the world.
Here I stand,
the proud father? – not me.
I have been utterly humbled
by your arrival.
You're not my offspring,
not part of me,
and yet, at the same time,
already inextricably part of my life.
I was your hasty midwife,
who delivered you with
unskilled trembling hands.
Who pulled you from your haven
into this.
The place which is more accustomed
to witnessing
the first uncertain breaths of
calves and lambs
than the first uncertain
breaths of a Messiah.
Here I stand with
your weight both
small and immense
resting on me.
So maybe I am proud,
proud of the privilege,
proud of being your father
just for the present.
And I pray, little Lord,
that just as I delivered you,
you will in return one day
deliver me.

Lisa Debney

I WAS THERE

I was there
in the stable
at Bethlehem.

Though you won't
see me
on Christmas cards.
Noble horses,
gentle cows
and cuddly lambs –
yes.

Rats?
No.

It wouldn't
be nice.
It would be like
blood
on a crucifix.

But when the snooty horses,
clumsy cows
and stupid sheep
had finished,
me and the missis
(should I say my 'partner and I'?)
looked in the manger.

The baby
smiled at us.

And I reckon
if the hyenas and snakes,
the spiders and toads,
the vultures and cockroaches
had arrived,
he would have smiled at them too.

Brian Ford

TO THE BABY GOD

(Tune: Brahms' Lullaby)

You are dearer than death,
you are gentler than breathing,
in the smallness of being,
in the nearness of you,
in the movement of limbs,
in the stillness of sleeping,
in the anguish of care,
is the wonder of you.

You are precious to me,
there is nobody like you;
every day holds delight
as I greet it with you.
What the future will bring
I have no way of telling,
but I trust you to show me
all the wonder of you.

I am filled with such awe
for I know my own weakness.
How can I do what's best
for the treasure of you?
But you give me your love
without question or doubting
so I know you'll forgive,
that's the wonder of you.

Go to sleep now my darling,
even you need your resting;
I will care by your side
for the world that you love.
You have given your life,
so frail and so trusting,
into my human hands,
that's the wonder of you.

Kathy Galloway

SOMEONE TO WATCH OVER
A sequence of meditations*

Mary

Does love's protection
always feel this fierce?
It is an aching in this
post-birth quiet, beautiful and yet
almost too strong to bear.

There is a jealousy of passion
in my soul that will not part
with what my body has birthed,
is frightened by the way you lie
alone, cut off and unprotected.

And even gathered close to me,
I cannot seem to hold you close enough
to keep the sense of night's weight
from pressing down on us
with something like foreboding.

I wrap my arms around you
and it hurts to feel the strength
of love that swells within my
throat and heart.

This will not cease,
this painful vigil
born of love.

But holding you pressed close
is worth the sharp, sad joy
of having heaven's
love and sorrow
lying quiet by my side.

Lamb

It was born too soon.

The keen night air
cut across the dampness of its body,
causing it to tremble and
shudder violently,
smacked by the roughness of new life.

Robbed of its mother's life-force,
its knees buckled and it hit the earth
and sank against the ground.
Small breaths it made
like it was only playing lightly with life.
Small breaths lifting the loose-fitting skin.

I placed it close against my chest,
as is our way with orphan lambs,
to preserve the last remains
of womb-warmth held inside.
It seemed to me a certainty
that this would be a life to ebb away
when sucked at by the coldness
of the clear night sky

But as we lay, the lamb and I,
side by side and sheltered
by the solid ancient forms of sheep,
I felt it stir as if to make
a protest over death itself.

And still I can remember
the way its life-blood pulsed with mine,
hotter and more vital
than the glowing embers
of that evening's fire.

Joseph

My arm around your back
was all that I could offer as support,
as each unravelling chapter came.

My arm around your back was there
when you first heard the news
that heaven dwelt in you,
and words fled faster from me
than response.
My arm around your back
was all that I could offer you
to reassure you that I would never desert.

My arm around your back
was all that I could offer as support
on Bethlehem's weary road,
as the journey wound round path and street
and doors closed swiftly in our faces.
My arm around your back was all I had
to protect you from despair.

As the child emerged in an open barn,
my arm around your back
was all I had to help you through.

To be a leaning post,
it seemed, was all that I could do
to show I struggled with you
in the birth.

It doesn't seem enough for one
who's destined to endure so much.
I should have words and eloquence or
money, land and powers of protection
that would buffer you
against the harshness of this world.

But all that I can offer is my arm around your back.
Its strength will never be enough to show
the strength of love that holds me to your side.
But ready still to comfort, to steady and to reassure,
my arm around your back, if needed, will be there.

Kings – Wisdom

Don't call me wise.
It isn't wisdom that
drives a man to leave
his home and travel
through the dead of night.

It isn't wisdom
that makes a man
leave all he has behind,
courts and comfort,
respect and standing,
to pursue a dream.

Don't call me wise.
I am not sure that
wisdom is a burden
that I want to own.

I've spent my life in study,
mapping charts,
recording information.
I am old in knowledge,
stale with information
held too long.

Don't call me wise.
Wisdom does not cause a man
to embrace adventure quite so fully.
It is a force apart from reason,

so far beyond himself
he doesn't know how to resist its call.

Don't call me wise.
It is not wise to reach out for the unattainable.
It is not wise to hold out so much hope.
It is not wise to feel this excited.

Am I following or chasing?
Am I looking for kings?
Or looking for meaning?

Drawn on by the magnetism of the future
I am shedding wisdom with each eager step.

I feel again the child's desire
to touch a star.

To touch the rim of heaven.

King – Stars

When I was young
I used to watch the
stars for hours on end.
I'd gaze so long that
when I turned my head away
the patterns of the constellations
still burned bright,
their outlines scorched
in shining traceries onto my mind.

And if I closed my eyes
the darkness in my head
became my own night sky,
and I could hold the universe,
controlling galaxies with ease
that only a child can know.

I owned each star
and watched its progress
whilst it swam through time,

as if it shone exclusively for me.
I came to know the intricacies of each journey,
travelling alongside each one in my thoughts.

Over the years the stars grew further away
as my knowledge increased.
I ceased trying to inhabit the infinite,
turned my back on vastness
to protect me from its scale.

What made me raise my eyes again?
Return to gazing,
fall in love once more
with the night sky's grandeur?

I own one star now,
watch its progress
with such closeness
you would think it shone
exclusively for me.

I watch so long
that when I close my eyes
it remains,
a single pin prick
burning in my mind.

All heaven has become
an intimate infinity,
choosing to dwell
behind a closed eyelid.

King – Anticipation

One more night. That's all we should have left. Just one more night.
It is nearer now.

We are resting before the final journey. I cannot sleep.

Something in the air is making the hair on the back on my neck stand on end.
My fingers are prickling with more than just the cold.
With each sharp breath I can taste excitement.

It is as if anticipation has just revealed itself to have a flavour
more pungent than any spice.

If I breathe out I can see my breath hanging in the air
and it gives me a child's delight to watch the invisible take on form.

I am laughing like a child. I cannot help myself.

Every sense heightened. Returned to its original vividness.

Tonight I can taste atmosphere, breathe sounds.

Tonight is such a young night.

And in it I am young too, younger than I have ever been.

I hear voices in the air:

the rustlings of angels,

the spreading of wings …

There is only one more night.

The invisible will take on form.

There is a promise hanging in the air.

I am breathing it in deep.

I cannot sleep.

Someone to watch over (closing prayer)

Joseph watching over Mary,
shepherds watching over sheep,
angels watching over shepherds,
kings watching over stars,
stars watching over kings …

And overseeing all is God,
watching over everything,
sheltering all under his outstretched wing.

The hand that rests on Mary's shoulder is God's.
The life-giving heat transferring from shepherd to lamb is God's.
The tender pain of realisation as Mary looks on her newborn son is God's.

The Christmas story tells of the care and protection that goes on at the expense of comfort. Extravagant gestures of compassion carried out at the expense of individuals because they are compelled to care through the sheer strength of love existing within them.

They are each an echo of God's love.
We are each an echo of God's love.

May you receive protection and care this Christmas.
May you have the chance to offer protection and care to others.
May you return to a childlike wonder
and be inspired to consider the infinite possibilities the sky might hold for you.
And, above all, may you know that you are sheltered under God's wing,
that he is watching over you tonight and all the nights to come.
Amen

Lisa Debney

These meditations were used in an informal, café setting. Live and recorded music was used, as well as dance and video-projected images.

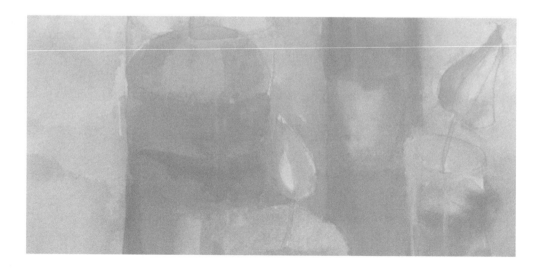

THE MARY OF YOUR CHRISTMAS CARDS

I am the Mary of your Christmas cards. I listen calmly while the angel brings me news that will shake my life beyond all measure. I accept what has been ordained for me. I am young and dressed in blue.

I am the Mary of your Christmas cards. Despite travelling almost 100 miles on a donkey across a desert and giving birth in a stable, I am still immaculately clean and tidy, cradling my infant son, unperturbed by my surroundings. I am still young and dressed in blue.

I am the Mary of your Christmas cards, welcoming shepherds from the nearby fields and strangers from afar; a person who treats such events as if they happened every day, calmly pondering on them in my heart. I am still young and dressed in blue.

But is this really me? Do you have any picture of me beyond that of Christmas cards?

Where is your picture of me in the temple, as Simeon tells me how a sword would pierce my soul? The angel brought greetings and told me not to be afraid, so I am calm on your Christmas cards; but do you never see the terror in my eyes as I hear Simeon's haunting words and I *do* fear what is to come?

Maybe you do have a picture of me 12 years later – but have I aged in your eyes? Am I calm and serene, frantically searching for my son, lost on return from the temple? He was calm – but not I. I was frantic.

Do you have a picture of me 30 years after your first picture of me? Am I still dressed in blue? Are there lines on my face? Is my hair now grey?

Do you see me at the wedding feast, recognising deep within that his time was coming and he would soon be no longer mine?

Do you see me hurt by his rejection when he declared that all the world was his mother and his brother and his sister. I knew that he had a greater purpose – but do not imagine that there was no pain for me in this.

How I aged in those three years. But am I still young in your picture? Was I not grey-haired as I stood at the foot of the cross? Do you know what it takes to watch your son being crucified? Some parents still do. As they pierced his side, my soul, too, was pierced. Do you have a picture of me – in tears, distraught at the anguish of my son? Or am I still the Mary of your Christmas cards?

They laid him in the tomb – it seemed so final – it seemed I had lost him for ever. Where was the angel now to tell me not to be afraid? My fellow countrywomen kept vigil; I was not alone in mourning. But you who know what happened next, do you let me grieve for the end I thought he'd reached?

You know the end – you know the triumph of his resurrection, the Kingdom without end – and knowing this affects your picture of me. I remain always young and dressed in blue, calm and serene, humble and willing – never allowed to show fear, hurt, anger, pain and grief.

For many, I remain the Mary of Christmas cards.

If I am to be called blessed, please remember all I stand for. As you receive your cards this Christmas, please look at me and remember that this is just the beginning.

Katie Baker

THEOTOKOS* – BROKEN DREAMS
Luke 1:26–56; 2:1–20; Matthew 2:1–15

Is this what you had in mind Mary?
Is this what you dreamed of,
idly planned and chattered of with the girls in Nazareth?
Did you dream that your first child would be
born out of wedlock
of an unknown father?
Born miles from home
in a place fit only for animals?
Is this the birth you dreamed of for your first child?

Did you dream your firstborn son would be
greeted by strangers?
Greeted by shepherds,
outcasts of society?
Greeted by wise men
from strange far-off countries?
Greeted by the host of angels?
Is this the welcome you dreamed of for your son?

Did you dream of this life for your firstborn son?
A birth in a stable?
A desperate flight for safety?
A life as a refugee?
A peripatetic life?
A life in which other women cared for him?

A life with no wife, no family?
A life lived in the shadow of hostility?
A life ending in a criminal's death?
A horrific death?
Is this the life you dreamed of for your son?

Did you dream of your own life?
A happy marriage?
A growing family?
Sons and daughters to care for you in your old age?
Did you dream of this for your own life?

And if you had known, in those days of idle teenage chatter,
as a girl in Nazareth,
what you know now,
would you have said 'yes' to God's angel so quickly?

Mary, did you say 'yes' to God's angel so quickly?
Did you offer yourself to God so fast?
Was there no feeling of wanting to think?
No sense of anger, injustice even,
that God could take your body and life so easily?
Did you really understand all that was being said?
All that was being asked?
And would I have been so willing?

Would I have been so willing
to offer myself to bear God's Son?
To bear the shame and disgrace
of bearing a child of an unknown father outside of marriage?
Would I have watched my own son die?
Would I have lived with the wound of knowledge,
a sword which pierced my heart?
Would I have lived with the burden of unknowing?
I doubt it.

Thank you, Mary, that you did.
You heard and looked, observed and listened.
Lived with the pain of unknowing.
Lived with the shadow of the cross.

Not as a stained glass window saint,
not as some saccharine-coated statue,
but as a flesh-and-blood woman
who knew what it meant
to bear the burden of unknowing,
and was prepared to live the pain
of bearing God.

Anne Lawson

Theotokos means 'God-bearer', and is usually applied to Mary in the Orthodox tradition.

NATIVITY

Incarnate Christ,
be born in me this Christmas!

May my will be as Mary's,
saying 'yes' to your ways;
my mind as Joseph's,
open to your unfolding revelation.

May my voice be as the angels',
joyfully proclaiming Good News;
my knees as the animals',
quietly bent in adoration.

May my feet be as the shepherds',
running eagerly to find you;
my hands as the wise men's,
offering up all that I have.

May my heart be as the manger,
poor yet containing heaven's greatest treasure;
my life as the stable,
hallowed and expanded by your presence.

Incarnate Christ,
be born again in me this Christmas!

Pat Bennett

STAY MY CHILD

Words: Anna Briggs. Music: Daniel Charles Damon.

Stay, my child, my body sharing.
Girlhood's peace from me is torn;
well I know a mother's fearing,
hope miscarried, joy stillborn.
Lullaby, lullaby,
God has heard a mother's cry, lullaby.

Grow, my child, in body chosen
by the God who made the earth;
mine the answer, in confusion,
young, unready to give birth.
Lullaby, lullaby,
God has heard a mother's cry, lullaby.

Sleep, my child, for love surrounds us,
we have not been left alone.
Though disgrace and shame may hound us,
Joseph stays and shields his own.
Lullaby, lullaby,
God has heard a mother's cry, lullaby.

Wake, my child; the world is crying,
calls you evil's power to cross;
opens you to early dying,
motherhood's most dreaded loss.
Lullaby, lullaby,
God has heard a mother's cry, lullaby.

Go, my child, God's grace protect you,
shape your living, fill your breath;
by its power to resurrect you,
break the grip of fear and death.
Lullaby, lullaby,
God has heard a mother's cry, lullaby.

Anna Briggs

CHRISTMAS SEEN

A saviour was born … light cleaving darkness.
Jesus! Ye were a wee bit early.
It's now yer needed,
these days the darkness is really frightening.
But you came tae save oor souls, no the world.
Izat right? … 'Cause if it's not … you should know
the world's jacket's on a shaky nail.

You want tae see whit they've done tae yer birthday!
I've read ye didnie laugh much
but ye'd laugh yerself silly at this –
rapacious greed wrapped in tinsel;
naive yearnings, struggling, stumbling,
mugged in the alleyways of commerce.

Actually … you're not that well-remembered –
red, red robin's more in evidence than you.
Santa Claus has hijacked the whole thing.
Mind you, he's a saint or something
so maybe that's aw right.

But don't despair … no'everybody
swallos plum pudding platitudes; I don't,
dentures deny me such delectation.

Every day's Christmas tae me.
Every morning yer born in my heart,
though every single night I go tae bed
having caused yer crucifixion.
But you're a realist … you'll understand that.
… Maybe someday …

Stuart Barrie

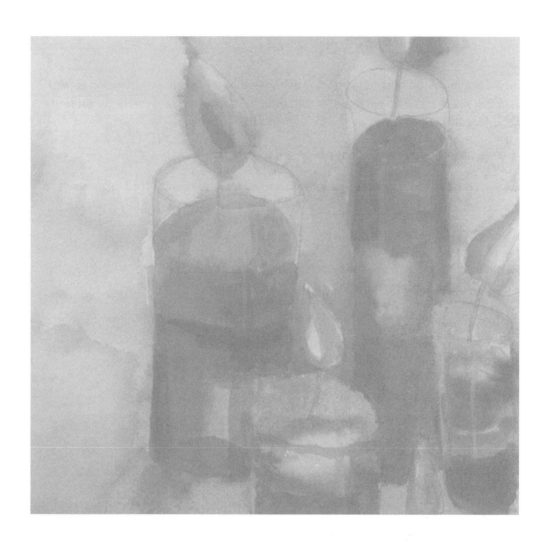

BIRTH

IN THE FULLNESS OF TIME

Lord God, in the fullness of time you took the ultimate risk. It was make or break. This frail life in a stable was your life knit with ours. You staked everything on one gambler's throw.

Had we been God we would have been wiser.

We would have had more respect for our own name and dignity, and taken steps to preserve it.

We would have made sure that a way of escape was kept open.

We give you thanks, you-with-us, Emmanuel, that you chose us, that you accept our lot, that you hold nothing back.

We bless you from full hearts that you are God and not us, that it is on you, rather than on us, that the future of creation depends.
The wisdom of God is wiser than our wisdom.
The weakness of God is stronger than our strength.
Thanks be to God most high. Amen

Ian M Fraser

A RUMOUR OF CHRISTMAS

Is this the moment
when the cosmic wonders of starlight
and the little beauties of candlelight
might touch the minds of the few
with incomprehensible longings
and trust in transience – almost hidden
by the vanity of tinsel and fairy lights,
the false strength of neon lights,
the deceptive durability
of plastic tree and moon-cold bauble?

Is this the moment
when a birth and a promise
put out the brash lights
and the pale trash,
let in the rumour:
a whisper of joy,
a faint flicker of hope,
a murmur of angels singing
for shepherds and war-worn travellers,
kings and troubled bishops,
Mary, and all women
who, in the bleakness of winter,
worship with a kiss?

Joy Mead

A WORK IN PROGRESS

Christmas child,
you stand at our stable door,
bearing the unwrapped gift
of terrible, unrelenting love.

You will us to be born
again, again and again.

Jim Hughes

GOD MADE LIFE

God made life!

That life was passed on through millions of years by genes – the same life shared by all living creatures from the first primeval DNA.

Through millions of generations and gradual genetic changes, God created women and men.

Then, through the human genetic chain, those genes brought life through the generations, until the Creator came and shared the life he had created – inhabited that same gene bank that had been passed down through Adam and Eve from the first life.

The recycled atoms that made up Jesus's body may have been part of dinosaurs, giant tree ferns, microscopic sea creatures, mud slime, glorious flowers or birds … The atoms might have been part of the prophets who called the people to God, or part of one of the kings who led them into all sorts of evil.

God – totally incarnate in his genes, in his atoms, in a living matrix with all of creation, from his family in Nazareth to a butterfly in the Amazon, from a Nazi guard to Mother Teresa, from that first life to you and me.

Frances Hawkey

MEDITATION IN FRONT OF THE CHURCH OF THE NATIVITY IN BETHLEHEM

A massive church
to hide a mucky wee stable.

Piles of books
to conceal the shocking simplicity.

Glorious works of art
to cover over the indescribable event.

Hymns galore sung by millions
to drown out a baby's crying.

Why do we always
have to find ways
of getting it wrong?

Ian Cowie

A NEW ME

Jesus,
born of woman,
you entered time.

Giver of life,
come,
change my darkness into light.

Breathe in me,
enter my heart.
I need you day by day.

Bring me to a new birth,
a new life,
a new me.

I want to be your child of light.
Please come.

Sarah Pascoe

IT'S CHRISTMAS

It's Christmas,
and everywhere are goodies –
piled high, overflowing –
glittering trinkets of modernity
submerging us,
imprisoning our souls,
offering us a transient joy.

Yet in
silent places of the heart
we rebel –
longing for that
inner freedom of the Spirit
which came
with the first Christmas,
and can transform
us still.

We touch
these gifts beyond price,
and, awakening to
the sacred within us,
experience again
that surprising,
tender love
which – centuries ago –
the shepherds encountered
in the midst of their work,
on those dry fields
near Bethlehem.

Peter Millar

WHAT GLORY THIS?

Metre: Long metre 8.8.8.8.

What glory this that angels sing
To frightened shepherds in the night,
News of God's son who comes to bring
Such peace as puts our fear to flight?

What glory this that dares be born
Into a suffering, broken world,
Yet sees the wonder of the dawn
And shows earth's beauty new unfurled?

What glory this that dares to cry
And share in all our human pain?
What glory that dares even die
To make creation whole again?

This is the glory of our God
Who, with a love that knows no bounds,
Intends to work till earth and heaven
With glory, joy and praise abound.

David Fox

CHRISTMAS COMING

This Christmas, Lord,
take a corner of my life
and steal in …
invade the busyness of my doing
with the quiet of your coming.

This Christmas, Lord,
take a corner of my mind
and steal in …
illuminate the darkness of my thinking
with the brightness of your seeing.

This Christmas, Lord,
take a corner of my heart

and steal in …
infuse the coldness of my loving
with the warmth of your Being.

This Christmas, Lord,
as at Bethlehem's stable,
come and steal in …
take the unprepared places of my life
and make them fit for your dwelling.

Pat Bennett

HUSH! WATCH! HEAR!

(A carol)

Words and tune: Ian M Fraser. Arranged by Donald Rennie.

Hush! Watch! Hear!
Something's in the air,
Age-old hopes
Seek fulfilment there:
Can it be – injustice,
Twisting life awry,
Will, in death defeated, lie?

Prick your ears –
May it be believed?
Suffering's
Now a gift received!
May the prayers and patience,
All the tears and pain,
Be converted to our gain?

Hold your breath,
Dare we think it true
That our race
May be made anew:
Twisted aspirations,
Turned from self and sin,
Letting life and wholeness in?

Rub your eyes –
Strange things are abroad,
See at work
Our surprising God:
Lays aside his glory,
Comes so weak and small –
Doesn't look like God at all.

Hush! Watch! Hear!
Something's in the air,
Age-old hopes
Seek fulfilment there –
Focus of all longings,
Hope of hopeful strife,
Is a tiny, human life!

Ian M Fraser

THE ROTARIAN CRIB

Coming up to Christmas,
Union Road resounded
to recorded carols from the Rotarians
(the real carol-singing happened elsewhere, for free).
Solid citizens shook their tins and stamped their boots,
glowing with goodwill in the frosty air,
and the passers-by coughed up.

There was a crib: a rustic stable
(courtesy of local firms)
and, behind a plastic screen,
the Holy Family full of pink-plaster piety,
nestled in real straw
(the real incarnation happened elsewhere).

There was also a Christmas tree,
with flashing lights
and a sign warning of mortal danger
if you touched it.
However, it was the nativity that touched
someone in the town, unaccountably,
for between Christmas and New Year
they grabbed the contents of the crib.

The carols faltered into silence,
for little Lord Jesus,
who had never cried anyway,
had stolen away.

Was it a massacre of the innocents?
The straw was an empty nest,
the plastic screen was rent in twain.
Was it a flight into Egypt or Stockport?
A Friday night trophy
more seasonal than traffic cones?
One thing is certain:
before The Year of the Family* ended,
the Holy Family had left town.

Jan Sutch Pickard

* This poem was written in 1994, which was designated 'The Year of the Family'.

CHRISTMAS IS A TIME FOR MY BELLY

Christmas is
When you can play games in the house
A time for my belly
The time when Father Christmas comes and you get toys
When everyone gets happy
When it's baby Jesus's birthday
When you can have a big dinner

Christmas is
When you get your mummy a present
When you have a cake and a pudding
For making things
The giving day
My favourite day
The nicest day of all

Christmas is
When you put up Christmas trimmings
When we play in the snow
When you get Christmas cards for people
When we sing carols
When you are very, very excited

Christmas is happy
Christmas is.

Written by a group of seven-year-olds

(Note: This is best read by a number of different voices.)

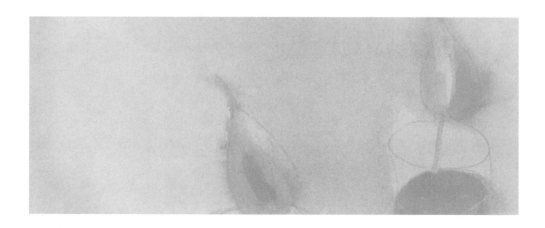

PROLOGUE

Inspiring Word,
move over the chaos within me,
calling forth form and order,
that I may know you in my shaping
and, in the shaping,
surrender my life to yours.

Illuminating Word,
pierce the darkness within me,
calling forth insight and understanding,
that I may know you in my seeing
and, in seeing,
follow the way of your Kingdom.

Incarnate Word,
indwell the life within me,
calling forth passion and purpose,
that I may know you in my living,
and, in living,
embody you for the world.

Pat Bennett

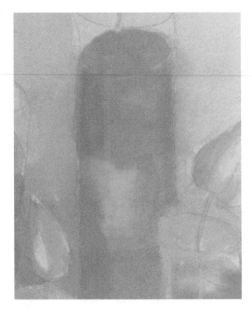

GIVE ME TEARS FOR CHRISTMAS

From the bairn in the byre
to the man on the cross
and the whole world between
a woman's tears were there

Mary the proud anxious girl
shedding tears of childbirth
Mary the bereaved anguished woman
shedding tears of grief
how little we know of her
how much she was one of us
how human she was
cradling the baby in her arms
cradling our Christ in her arms
turning the first page of the story
the book that is open still

O my God
give me this story for Christmas
show me the faith of Mary for Christmas
cradle me while the story unfolds
and if my faith one day grows dry
give me the gift of tears.

Andrew Foster

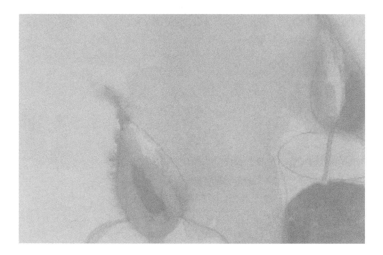

IN THE BEGINNING

Words and music: Carol Dixon

Cantor:	In the beginning was the Word *(All repeat)*
Cantor:	and the Word was with God. *(All repeat)*
ALL:	IN THE BEGINNING WAS THE WORD
Cantor:	and the Word was God.

Cantor:	In the beginning all was dark *(All repeat)*
Cantor:	and the Word brought the Light. *(All repeat)*
ALL:	IN THE BEGINNING ALL WAS DARK,
Cantor:	but the Light still shines.

Cantor:	The Word of God came to his own *(All repeat)*
Cantor:	and his own knew him not. *(All repeat)*
ALL:	THE WORD OF GOD CAME TO HIS OWN,
Cantor:	and they turned away.

Cantor:	The Word of God was born on earth *(All repeat)*
Cantor:	to bring life to the world. *(All repeat)*
ALL:	THE WORD OF GOD WAS BORN ON EARTH
Cantor:	to bring life from God.

Cantor:	The Word became a human being *(All repeat)*
Cantor:	bearing likeness to God. *(All repeat)*
ALL:	THE WORD BECAME A HUMAN BEING,
Cantor:	full of grace and truth.

Cantor: One day the Word will come again *(All repeat)*
Cantor: bringing glory and peace. *(All repeat)*
ALL: ONE DAY THE WORD WILL COME AGAIN
Cantor: and will claim his own.

Cantor: Praise to the living Word of God *(All repeat)*
Cantor: the beginning and end. *(All repeat)*
ALL: PRAISE TO THE LIVING WORD OF GOD *(together)*
Cantor: who redeems the world.

Carol Dixon

THE WORD

The Word became
words,
millions of words,
tumbling off pages,
running across screens,
communicating,
explaining,
informing,
amusing,
tedious,
arguing,
pompous,
tentative,
authoritative,
confused,
hating,
loving.
The
Word
became
a human being.
The Word is in
the world.

Margaret Harvey

JESUS IS BORN

(Tune: The infant King)

Jesus is born!
Formed in a womb and now a baby.
Jesus is born!
Swaddled and small, he sleeps in hay.
Setting aside his power and glory,
Homeless he enters human story:
Christ comes to earth.

Jesus is born!
Angels announce a joyful message.
Jesus is born!
'Peace on the earth, goodwill to all –
This is the hour God shows his favour,
Sending his Son, creation's Saviour':
Hope comes to earth.

Jesus is born!
High overhead a star is shining.
Jesus is born!
Earth houses uncreated light.
Now is the hold of darkness broken
As hearts and minds to God are opened:
Light comes to earth.

Jesus is born!
This night the world is changed for ever.
Jesus is born!
And in this babe for all to see
Love is revealed; God's heart lies open
As the incarnate Word is spoken:
God comes to earth.

Pat Bennett

OCCASIONAL SIGHTINGS OF THE GOSPEL

When I am lonely,
wondering if I have a friend in the world,
it embraces me with its comfort;

when I am prone to ignore the world,
it pushes me into its delights;

when I wander the streets of today's culture,
it shadows me to keep me out of trouble;

when I think that I have no responsibilities
for those around me,
it grabs me and shakes me;

when I am broken by the suffering
of those I love,
it caresses me with its peace;

when I strut my arrogant pride,
it shatters me into humility;

whenever I need a Word
God provides it.

Thom M Shuman

CHRISTMAS BLESSING

The wisdom of the wonderful counsellor guide you,
the angels of the Lord of hosts guard you,
the strength of the mighty God uphold you,
the love of the everlasting Father enfold you,
the joy of the Prince of peace be yours,
this Christmastide and for ever.

Ian Cowie

NIGHT PRAYER WITH BLANKETS

Cradle us God;
fold us into your tears and laughter,
wrap us deep in love.

Cradle us God;
weave us into joy and justice,
hem us round with hope.

Cradle us God;
tumble us into questions and stories,
toss us up into joy.

Cradle us God;
rock us into rest and dreaming,
cuddle us into your peace.

Ruth Burgess

Written for Key House, a retreat house in Scotland, where they supply blankets in their chapel, which was once a stable.

CHRISTMAS IS WHEN I AM JOSEPH

Christmas is
When I can choose what I want for breakfast
When I am Joseph in a play
Ripping my presents open
Making a mess

Christmas is
When we light candles
When we sing in the choir
When we hang our stockings up
When my dad goes out for a drink

Christmas is
When I say a prayer
When we get a new dog's bed for Lucy
Bursting balloons
Having a nice dinner
Celebrating Jesus
Giving

Christmas is when the church bells ring
Christmas is.

Written by a group of 9-year-olds

(Note: This is best read by a number of different voices.)

LIGHT

O GLORIOUS GOD OF THE STARS

Words from the Carmina Gadelica. Music: Pat Livingstone

O glo - rious God of the stars _____ O glo - rious God of the

skies _____ O glo - rious God of the hea - vens _____

Blessed by You has been ev -'ry tribe and peo - ple. _____ ____ O __

Pat Livingstone

A THOUGHT

Dust
stardust
everything made of it

rocks
trees

elephants
plankton

stardust

you
me
Jesus
all of us
stardust

twinkle
twinkle

Wow

Ruth Burgess

INSIDE ME

Inside me darkness, light.
Inside me courage, fright.
Inside me at Christmastime,
working hard to clean the grime
of bells and sells and forged noels,
of glitter balls and sugar shells,
a small bright shoot bursts through the clay,
ignores the plum duff and buffet.
Through the darkness to the light,
unaffected by the blight,
nothing in its shopping cart,
waking up my sleeping heart,
shaking shadows from its fear,
igniting now Christ's chandelier.

Stuart Barrie

LIGHT TO YOUR PEOPLE

Lord Jesus,
we thank you
that when the world was very dark
you came
to bring light into our darkness.
You came in the night
to bring light into the lives
of Mary and Joseph.
You came to Bethlehem –
then, as now, a very troubled town –
bringing light to all
who came to trust you.

You come to us now,
into our lives
and into our world,
bringing light still to your people.

We ask you now
once again
to accept this worship
that we bring
as we come again
to the manger.

Help us to see there
the light that will shine for us,
not just at Christmas
but every day of the year.

John Harvey

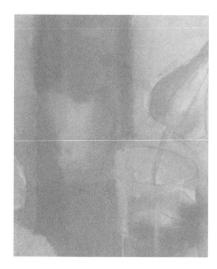

THANK YOU GOD

An all-age liturgy

(Arrange the seats in the worship space into a circle.)

Opening responses

God, Creator,
Sun maker,
Moon maker,
Star maker,
in love you made us.
Thank you God.
THANK YOU GOD.

God in Jesus,
Storyteller,
Healer,
Teacher,
in joy you came for us.
Thank you God.
THANK YOU GOD.

God here among us,
Comforter,
Listener,
Disturber,
in justice you beckon us.
Thank you God.
THANK YOU GOD.

A Christmas story *(appropriate to the ages of the people in the congregation)*

Prayers of intercession and lighting candles

Leader: Please end your prayer request with the words: 'God be with ...' So that we may respond: AMEN.

After all the candles are lit, the group say together:

ALL: GOD, CREATOR, STORYTELLER, LISTENER,
SEE OUR CANDLES; HEAR OUR PRAYERS.
HELP US TO BE LIGHT IN OUR WORLD,
TODAY AND EVERY DAY. AMEN

Blessing

Leader: In turn, round the circle, we hold the hands of our neighbour and say: 'God bless you.'

Closing responses

Now, as we blow out the candles (*time for this to happen*),
stay with us God.
STAY WITH US GOD.

Soon, as we say goodbye to each other,
stay with us God.
STAY WITH US GOD.

Always and everywhere, as we travel homewards,
stay with us God.
STAY WITH US GOD. AMEN

Ruth Burgess

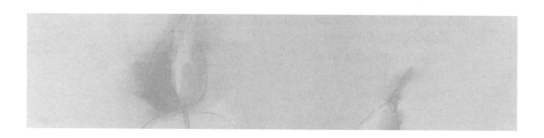

CHRISTMAS BY CANDLELIGHT

In a darkened room,
the child of the forties
smells guttering candles
clasped to the shadowy fronds
of a Christmas tree,
sees silk-spun baubles
and a tissue star.

The hardboard crib,
with straw-stuck roof,
attracts the child of the fifties,
who has placed before it
an opaque paper tube
in which a candle
burns dangerously.

Spinning metal angels,
hung above candle flames,
for a brief time span
give a sixties' twist
to the centrepiece.

A seventies' child
holds, in Christingle,
the juicy orange,
the red-trimmed ribbon,
the candlelight of the world.

Advent eighties
come and go,
while a layered, circled candle
burns the days,
dissolves the rings.

Sophisticated nineties' candles
float on reflecting pools.
The three ships
come sailing in.

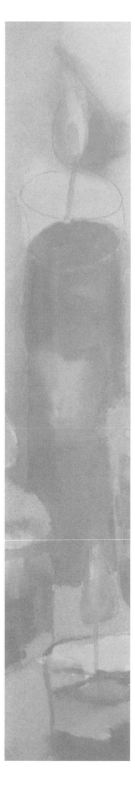

In this new century,
crafted candles
of myrrh and frankincense
perfume the air.

Symbols for storytelling,
candles for illumination,
speak to the child,
year on year

Margaret Moakes

LIGHT IN THE WORLD

Prayer for an all-age service

Lord Jesus,
you are the light of the world.
Shine in the dark places
where there are wars
and where people hurt each other.
Lord, in your mercy,
HEAR OUR PRAYER.

Lord Jesus,
you are the light of the world.
Help our leaders
to know how to run this country and this city
so that everybody's needs are met,
especially those who are suffering.
Lord, in your mercy,
HEAR OUR PRAYER.

Lord Jesus,
you are the light of the world.
Shine in the dark places
where people are ill or sad.
Please bring help and healing especially to …
Lord, in your mercy,
HEAR OUR PRAYER.

Lord Jesus,
we are your lights in the world.
Help us to be prepared
to show people your light
by loving them.
Lord, in your mercy,
HEAR OUR PRAYER.

Lord Jesus,
we are your lights in the world.
Help us to be prepared
to put the needs of others
before our own needs
for your sake.
Lord, in your mercy
HEAR OUR PRAYER.

Lord Jesus,
we are your lights in the world.
Help us to be prepared
to look out for you
and listen out for you
so we can follow you in everything we do.
Lord, in your mercy,
HEAR OUR PRAYER. AMEN

John Davies

(Used in an all-age service with The Guides. Six readers of different ages read a section of the prayer and then lit a candle. 'Be prepared to serve' is the motto of The Guides Association.)

PHOTO INTERCESSIONS

We pray for:

All whose pain has been reduced to a photograph in a newspaper, destined to be thrown away tomorrow.

All who feel frozen into a snapshot of themselves with no hope of escape.

All who feel their lives are posed, grin-fixed to conceal inner pain.

All whose lives seem as easily wiped of value as an image on a digital camera.

All whose anger bubbles like a Polaroid picture held over a flame.

All who sense their lives are out of focus or over-exposed.

All whose living seems as sepia and as ghostly as a photo from the distant past.

Dynamic God,
in whose image we are truly made,
hear our prayers.

Rachel Mann

CLOSING RESPONSES

Light of God
LEAD US

Power of God
HOLD US

Joy of God
HEAL US

Laughter of God
BLESS US

Love of God
CARESS US

Ruth Burgess

EMMANUEL

ISAAC'S CAROL

In 2003, Malvern Churches asked John L Bell if he would judge a carol-writing competition which was open to three age ranges – Primary School, Secondary School and Adults. Entries were to be set to a well-known Welsh carol tune.

Around 60 manuscripts were sent. There were a few good entries but nothing outstanding until John came across a supplementary batch at the back which consisted of material which didn't quite fit the bill, most often because it didn't go to the prescribed tune.

That was where Isaac's carol appeared.

It seemed a totally unaffected expression of love for Jesus, and it stood in stark contrast to everything else.

So John decided to give it first prize, even if it didn't meet all the criteria … and then discovered that the author didn't meet the criteria either, for Isaac Hutchings was only three and a half, too young even for the Primary class.

Isaac's mother wrote to say that there had been considerable interest in his achievement but Isaac couldn't understand why the newspapers and radio wanted to interview him. He just wanted to play … presumably at Bob the Builder.

Father God, I love you
and your little Jesus.
I would like to kiss him
and give him a cuddle.
I would share all my toys
and play lots of games with him.
Bob the Builder we could play;
we would be the best of mates.

Isaac Hutchings

Words: Isaac Hutchings. Tune: John L Bell.

Fa-ther God, I love you and your lit-tle Je - sus. I would like to kiss him and give him a cud - dle. I would share all my toys and play lots of games with him. Bob the Build - er we could play; **we** would be the best of mates.

EMMANUEL GOD

Words and music: David Coleman

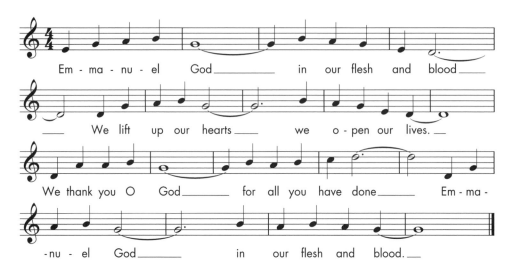

David Coleman

IMMANUEL: A LITURGY

Preparation

The seating for this service should be in a circle or horseshoe shape, with a large table placed in the centre of the worship space. On the table, set a simple Advent ring of four coloured candles with a fifth, larger white candle in the centre of the ring; small votive candles (enough for each person in the congregation); and tapers or plenty of long matches. Have a small candle already lit on the table.

If possible, spend time before worship learning the canticle and making sure people understand what is going to happen in the service.

Play music to set the mood.

Opening responses and grounding in scripture

(The words below marked 'Reader' can be shared by two or three leaders or by individuals in rotation around the circle. All the text in capital letters is spoken by the congregation.)

Reader: God is with us!
IMMANUEL!

Reader: God said to Jacob, in a vision of angels, 'Know that I am with you and will keep you wherever you go ...' *(Genesis 28:15)*
IMMANUEL!

Reader: God said to the people of the covenant, 'Do not fear, for I am with you, do not be afraid, for I am your God; I will strengthen you, I will help you.' *(Isaiah 41:10)*
IMMANUEL!

Reader: The prophet Isaiah recorded the words of God: 'Look, the young woman is with child and shall bear a son, and shall name him Immanuel (that is, *God with us*).' In that young woman we see Mary, and in Immanuel, her son, our Christ. *(Isaiah 7:14)*
GOD IS WITH US!

Reader: Of John the Baptist it was said, 'And you, child, will be called the prophet of the Most High; for you will go before the Lord to prepare his ways ... by the tender mercy of our God, the dawn from on high will break upon us.' *(Luke 1:76,78)*
GOD IS WITH US!

Reader: 'And remember,' said Jesus, 'I am with you always, to the end of the age.' *(Matthew 28:20)*
GOD IS WITH US!

Reader: And of the New Heaven and New Earth it is written, 'See, the home of God is among mortals. He will dwell with them as their God ... he will wipe every tear from their eyes. 'It is done! I am the Alpha and Omega, the beginning and the end.' *(Revelation 21:1–6)*
GOD IS WITH US!
IMMANUEL!

Canticle *(repeat twice)*

Music: Annie Heppenstall-West

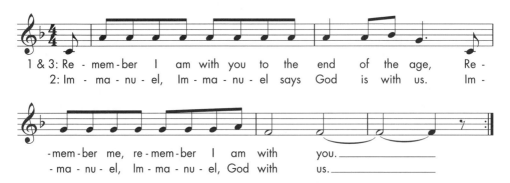

1 & 3: Re - mem - ber I am with you to the end of the age, Re -
2: Im - ma - nu - el, Im - ma - nu - el says God is with us. Im -

-mem - ber me, re - mem - ber I am with you._____
-ma - nu - el, Im - ma - nu - el, God with us._____

Prayer of reconciliation

Reader: Holy One, when we reject people because we see only faults,
we miss Immanuel.

When we condemn, isolate, belittle, look down on those we see as failing,
we miss Immanuel.

WHEN WE FAIL TO ENTER INTO THE DESPERATION OF ANOTHER,
WHEN WE CANNOT EMPATHISE,
WHEN OUR COMPASSION DIES WITHIN US,
THEN WE FAIL TO RECOGNISE IMMANUEL.

Reader: When the imagination dries up in our hearts,
when we cannot support others in their struggles to stand up,
then we fail to recognise Immanuel.

MAKE US WARM TO THE POTENTIAL IN OTHERS,
AND GIVE THEM SAFE SPACE TO BIRTH, TO GROW,
TO LIVE OUT THEIR GOD-GIVEN LIVES.
LET US EMBRACE THE TRUTH OF IMMANUEL,
AND SO FIND GOD WITH US.
AMEN

Canticle *(as above)*

The lighting of the Advent ring

Reader: Mary, overcome by the Spirit of God, knew that within her grew something holy, something to be cherished. For that knowledge she was brought low in the eyes of her community, and suffered.
YET GOD WAS WITH HER, AND WITHIN HER, AND GOD EXALTED HER.

A candle is lit by the reader.

BLESSED ARE YOU WHEN PEOPLE HATE YOU,
AND WHEN THEY EXCLUDE YOU, REVILE YOU,
AND DEFAME YOU ON ACCOUNT OF THE SON OF MAN.
REJOICE IN THAT DAY AND LEAP FOR JOY,
FOR SURELY YOUR REWARD IS GREAT IN HEAVEN. *(Luke 6:22–23)*

Reader: Elizabeth, filled with the wisdom of God's Spirit, knew that God weaves meaning and purpose into life. She embraced Mary in the pain of her loneliness and vulnerability, and rejoiced in her unborn child of God.
GOD WAS WITH THEM, AND WITHIN THEM.

A candle is lit by the reader.

BLESSED ARE YOU WHO WEEP NOW, FOR YOU WILL LAUGH.
(Luke 6:21b)

Reader: Joseph, in his humble openness to the Word of God, knew that he must defy convention to honour God's will. The shamed mother must be affirmed in her motherhood, the fatherless child accepted and given the chance to live and grow as one of God's people.
HE DARED TO GIVE SAFE SPACE, SANCTUARY,
IN WHICH GROWTH INTO FULLNESS COULD TAKE PLACE.
GOD SPOKE TO HIM.

A candle is lit by the reader.

WOE TO YOU WHEN ALL SPEAK WELL OF YOU,
FOR THAT IS WHAT THEIR ANCESTORS DID TO THE FALSE PROPHETS.
(Luke 6:26)

Reader: John the Baptist, who proclaimed to the world the imminence of Immanuel, used this prophecy: 'Every valley shall be lifted up and every mountain and hill shall be made low; the uneven ground shall become

level, and the rough places a plain. Then the glory of the Lord will be revealed ...' *(Isaiah 40:4)*
HE DARED TO FORSAKE ALL, GIVING HIMSELF AS A VOICE OF GOD,
A PROPHET PROCLAIMING THE TRUTH OF GOD'S CLOSENESS.

A candle is lit by the reader.

BLESSED ARE YOU WHO ARE POOR,
FOR YOURS IS THE KINGDOM OF HEAVEN ...
BUT WOE TO YOU WHO ARE RICH,
FOR YOU HAVE RECEIVED YOUR CONSOLATION. *(Luke 6:20, 24)*

Reader: Jesus came to give himself in love to the people, to be among them, knowing their troubles and meeting them there, each in their own wilderness, man and woman and child, raising them up or bringing them down, and showing them a path to tread, back to the true community of God's kingdom.
IN THE LOVE OF JESUS WE SEE AND KNOW THE TRUTH THAT GOD IS WITH US.

The central candle is lit by the reader.

Reader: He unrolled the scroll and found the place where it is written:
'The Spirit of the Lord is upon me,
Because he has anointed me
To bring good news to the poor,
He has sent me to proclaim release to the captives
And recovery of sight to the blind,
To let the oppressed go free.' *(Luke 4:17–18)*
IN COMPASSION AND LOVE IS GOD WITH US. AMEN

A time of quiet reflection with background music or silence, if preferred. During this time people are invited to come and light a votive candle and to place it on the table.

Reader: Let us, like Mary, endure criticism and rejection, if only to be pregnant with the life of God in us;
Reader: always waiting,
Reader: anticipating the day of birth,
Reader: the day when we see you and know you,
Reader: the day when we know God has burst through into our lives,

Reader: conceived within us, from a power beyond us …
THE DAY OF YOUR COMING INTO OUR LIVES.

Reader: Let us accept the truth:
GOD WITH US MEANS THE HUMBLING OF THE PROUD AND THE RAIS-
ING UP OF THE LOWLY.

Reader: Let us welcome the truth:
GOD WITH US MEANS FREEDOM FOR THE OPPRESSED AND RELEASE
FOR THE CAPTIVES.

Reader: Let us proclaim the truth:
GOD WITH US MEANS THE BREAKING THROUGH OF GOD'S DAWN,
INTO OUR SHADOW LIVES.

Reader: Let us rejoice in the truth:
GOD WITH US MEANS GOD DWELLS AMONGST US AND WITHIN US.

Reader: Let us look upon one another as houses of God's presence and so share
peace.

All share a sign of peace.

Repeat canticle

Reader: 'And remember,' said Jesus, 'I am with you always, to the end of the age.'

Reader: With us to show the way,
WITH US TO HEAL US,

Reader: With us to challenge us,
WITH US TO TEACH US AND STRENGTHEN US,

Reader: With us as we stumble into our wilderness,
AND WITH US AS WE FIND THE PATH HOME,

Reader: With us in our weakness and in our strength,
WITH US IN OUR DYING AND OUR RETURN TO LIFE.

The large white Christ-candle is lifted up.

Reader: So let us carry the light of Immanuel into the world,
walking where the Spirit guides us,
even into the dark places of the land.

Reader: The haunts of violence
and the places where the poor and needy are downtrodden and shamed;
the places where the rich and powerful have abused their position.

Reader: The margins and forgotten places,
the neglected and torn places,
the places where light must shine.

Reader: In the name of God, our Mother and Father,
in the name of Christ, Immanuel.
AMEN
GOD IS WITH US!
LET US CARRY THE LIGHT OF IMMANUEL IN OUR HEARTS AS WE GO
OUT INTO THE WORLD. AMEN

The large lighted candle is carried out to mark the end of the service. Each person is given a small unlighted candle to take home with them.

Annie Heppenstall-West
(with thanks to Ray, Steve, James, Isobel, Kate and Peter at All Hallows)

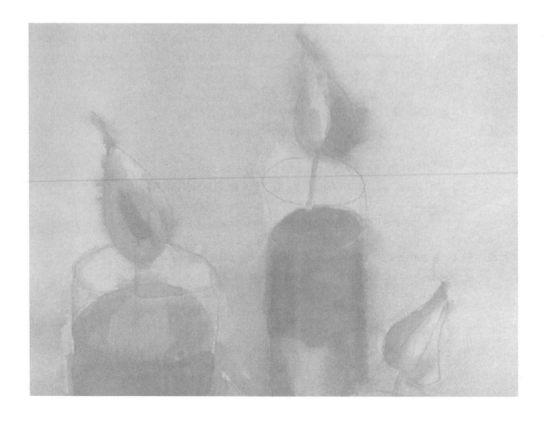

A SERIOUS CAROL

How horrible to go hungry at Christmas.
Lost, lonely, loveless, left behind,
Deprived, deformed, desolate and dying;
How awful, how unkind.

We cling to each other at Christmas,
Hunting for love to share,
Giving the simple presents,
The signs of care.

O that God's love would kindle
The candle of peace in our hearts,
And carry us out like angels
To smother sin's smart.

Robin Watt

BETHLEHEM 2002

Suppose he had been born today
in an occupied country.
Joseph would have telephoned for the ambulance
because it was her first
and they had nowhere to go.
The walls of the inn had been smashed by tanks
so they were hiding in the cellar.

The ambulance was shot at anyway,
two paramedics died.
No one came.
He was born, placed in an old basin.
There was no water –
a bomb had split the main.
He was wrapped in a dirty towel
still stiff with the innkeeper's blood.

Suppose the shepherds had tried to visit.
They wouldn't have got through the cordon.

Shot before they got close
in case their warm clothes were just a disguise
and they were intending to blow up the command post.
And the lamb would have been highly suspect.

The wise men from the east
would never have made it past Jerusalem.
Their camel train torn apart
in a search for illegal weapons.
Their gifts blown up
just in case they were booby-trapped.

And both sides would report
that missiles were fired from helicopter gun-ships
to counter a potential aerial assault.
The angels never stood a chance.

Alix Brown

HIDDEN JOURNEYS OF THE NATIVITY
A meditation

In this meditation, use a collection of Christmas cards and a copy of Rublev's icon of the nativity and look at the journeys they portray.

First of all, we might think of *Mary's journey* to Bethlehem. How did she travel? With excitement and expectancy, and also with anxiety and fear? She must have travelled with lots of questions, and probably also with exhaustion and physical pain.

Joseph's journey was a mixed one. He seems to have been caught in that place between faith and doubt – willing to be faithful in his commitment to Mary, but struggling to believe those things he couldn't understand.

The *shepherds' journey* was that of simple faith. They simply received the good news of the angels and responded.

The *wise men* travelled from far off. They were seized with wonder at the mysterious star and set out on a search – following, seeking, asking questions when they were lost. For them it was an intellectual journey, seeking to understand the signs in the heavens.

The *midwives* are almost always missing from our Christmas cards (though they appear in Rublev's icon of the nativity), but what an important role they served! They helped to bring light and love to birth. Their journey was one of compassionate care. They found God by tending to human need with love.

For reflection

☆   Think of your own spiritual journey this year.

☆   Do you feel close to any of the figures in the story, or identify with any of their different journeys?

☆   What have been the questions you have lived with?

☆   Have you known exhaustion and physical pain, and what does that do to your faith?

☆   What have you looked forward to with expectancy?

☆   What about being tempted to give up the struggle? Your moments of doubt?

☆   How have you felt far away from God?

☆   Can you name the moments of wonder that have nourished your journey?

☆   Where have you found God in your caring?

Prayer

In our journeying we find you,
God of the unexpected places.
We find you there – in our doubts
as well as our certainties,
in our fears as well as our courage,
in our questions as well as our wonder,
and in our turning to others to care.
Help us to journey on,
looking expectantly to find you.

Lynda Wright

A PRAYER AT CHRISTMAS

Help me to find that isolation in myself,
enabling me to see the lonely.

Help me to discover my vulnerability,
and find compassion for the child.

Help me to identify my frightened self,
and empathise with those for whom life is a daily torture.

Help me to understand the fear and anger,
which make me want to hurt and punish, and know something of the torturer.

Help me to discover that hidden part of me,
which is beyond the pale, rejected,
fearful, lonely, tired,
and in it recognise the refugee,
accept the stranger,
stand in another's shoes,
respond to all God's people. Amen

Jill Rhodes

TELLING THE STORY

The fire burns bright tonight,
frost whispers, the sky is eager with stars;
listen, once more the story is being told.
Listen, but who is doing the telling?
Is it prophets with foresight,
or Gospel writers with hindsight;
astrologers speaking in riddles,
or shepherds celebrating with bagpipes?

Is it angels cleaving the clouds
with unnerving presence,
with Godwords sung not said
and, like snowflakes, complex and unique?

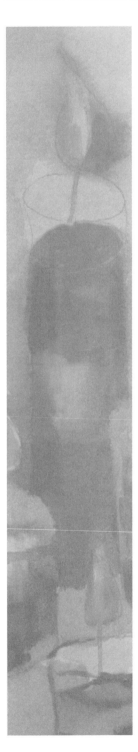

Is it common men, caught up
in something beyond comprehension,
stammering the story
in words wholly down-to-earth?

Is it the magi, for all their measured words,
giving away the intelligence Herod needs?
Is it Mary, silent as snowfall,
keeping these keen-edged things
and turning them over in her heart?
Is it Simeon's benediction and proclamation
or Anna gossiping the good news?
The fire burns bright tonight,
frost whispers, the sky is eager with stars;
listen, once more the story is being told.

It has been written out over and over again,
with the patient rhythms of a pen;
painted like a jewel on vellum;
carved in dark oak, chiselled in pale stone;
glimpsed in a bright window, gazing back from an icon;
read solemnly from the big book on the eagle's back;
acted with laughter in the market place,
or danced to the lilt of a carol.
The fire burns bright tonight,
frost whispers, the sky is eager with stars;
listen, once more the story is being told.

Reading the headlines, talking across a table,
we hear it happening still,
in places both familiar and far:
in croft, and Gorbals flat and West Bank stable,
and starting where we are.
This is the story that we need to tell –
God down-to-earth, with us, Immanuel.

Jan Sutch Pickard

LIFE AND LOVE

In a world that is lost –
SHOW US THE WAY.

In a world full of lies and deceit –
SHOW US THE TRUTH.

In a world that is sick and decayed –
SHOW US LIFE AND LOVE.

O JESUS, HELP US TO REMEMBER
THAT YOU ARE THE WAY, THE TRUTH AND THE LIFE,
ON CHRISTMAS DAY AND EVERY DAY. AMEN

Cath Threlfall

OUR NEEDS AND THOSE OF OTHERS

Loving God,
the gospel stories have become so familiar over the years
that we accept them almost unthinkingly.
Grant that we may be open to their shock value
as well as to the comfort of the news they bring.
We pray that we may see the relevance of them to life today,
and may extend our compassion to those whose stories resonate with yours.

We pray for pregnant women,
as new life grows within.
We hold before you their hopes and fears,
the anticipation of pain,
and the expectation of joy.
We think especially of those who have not chosen their state,
who wonder how they will cope,
who are unsure about the father,
who wonder about the reaction of family and friends.
May they find reassurance and acceptance.

We pray for fathers to be,
wondering about the part they should play,

who fear responsibility and commitment,
who are tempted to run away.
May they find encouragement and affirmation.

We pray for those who cannot have children,
to whom the story of Mary's cousin Elizabeth
must seem all at once hopeful, far-fetched and frustrating.
May they find hope and inspiration.

We pray for the mighty who have fallen:
those who have had power wrenched from them,
whether through democratic or violent means;
those who have lost wealth,
whether through bad judgement or failed enterprise;
those whose pride has been dented,
whether in public or private.
May they find hope and renewal.

Giving thanks for those whose lives have changed for the better,
we pray for those who still need to be lifted up,
who are hungry and need good things.
We pray for those who are denied basic freedoms,
who are denied housing, healthcare and education.
May they hear and trust in your promises.

As we go about our daily lives may we, like Mary,
treasure our experiences and ponder them in our hearts,
holding before you our own needs and those of others,
praising you and giving thanks.
For the sake of the Christ child, all that he is and was and shall be. Amen

Liz Gibson

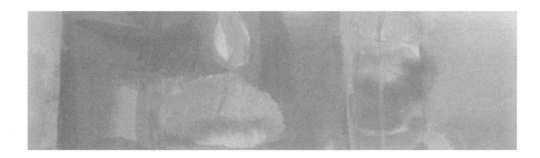

CHILD OF BETHLEHEM

We come before you, Christmas child, in silent amazement.
May we welcome you among us.
Child of Bethlehem,
HEAR OUR PRAYERS.

As Mary welcomed you and rejoiced in God's holiness and mercy,
we pray for the church as Christmas approaches.
Child of Bethlehem,
HEAR OUR PRAYERS.

As shepherds welcomed you, disturbing their work and lives,
we pray for your disturbing presence in our world.
Child of Bethlehem,
HEAR OUR PRAYERS.

As Joseph welcomed you, giving you a home and a name,
we pray for all who seek shelter in our community today/tonight ...
Child of Bethlehem,
HEAR OUR PRAYERS.

As angels welcomed you, singing of glory and peace,
we pray for all who seek healing and hope.
Child of Bethlehem,
HEAR OUR PRAYERS.

As Simeon welcomed you, recognising in you his journey's fulfilment,
we pray for those who have died and for all who love them and miss them ...
Child of Bethlehem,
HEAR OUR PRAYERS.

As wise men welcomed you, risking a journey and following a star,
we pray that we may take risks in following you.
Child of Bethlehem,
HEAR OUR PRAYERS.

The love of God is in us:
The spirit of joy is with us,
Emmanuel,
Jesus,
now and always. AMEN

Ruth Bowen

CHRISTMAS REFLECTION WRITTEN WITH CHILDREN AND YOUNG PEOPLE

Let's take a break for a few minutes to think about what Christmas means – the celebration and the sadness, the thankfulness and the pain.

We give thanks for the many gifts and presents we receive … And we remember the people who haven't got the money to buy material things.

We give thanks for the warmth, bright lights, and Christmas trees in our homes … And we remember the people who are living on the streets this Christmas.

We give thanks for the times we have together with friends and family … And we remember the people who are lonely, or who are spending Christmas alone.

We give thanks for the memories of good times we have had in the past … And we remember those for whom this time is painful because they have lost someone close to them.

We give thanks for the gift of Jesus and for all the joy of belonging in the church … And we remember the people who have not heard or understood the message of God's love in Jesus.

Jan Berry

SOMETIMES I CRY

(Tune: Summertime)

Sometimes I cry when I think of the child,
born in a stable, no room anywhere,
growing to live in a world cold with grief and shame,
dying in agony, nailed there by fear.

Sometimes I pray when I think of the child,
born to be human in weakness and care,
growing to stand with the poor and the prisoner,
dying to raise them in freedom to share.

Sometimes I laugh when I think of the child,
born without name on the edge of the town,
growing in powerlessness, changer of images,
dying derided and mocked as a clown.

Sometimes I tremble when I think of the child,
born out of mystery, starlight and sign,
maker of miracles out of reality,
raising them up till the end of all time.

But sometimes I sing when I think of the child,
born out of joy and obedience and pain,
growing to touch human living with ecstasy,
dying to show us that love lives again.

Kathy Galloway

PRAYER FOR CHILDREN

Thank you, living God,
that you dared to come to us
in the child Jesus,
that you took the risk
of being vulnerable and dependent.
We pray today for
justice for children.
That throughout the world
they may live without fear of war,
have their daily needs met,
and grow realising your gifts
hidden within them.

Lord, in your mercy,
HEAR OUR PRAYER.

We pray today
for faith for children.
For their spirits to grow
to know and love you – their Creator.
Bless those whose spirits are stunted
from poverty or mindless wealth;
may they know your purpose for them.

Lord, in your mercy,
HEAR OUR PRAYER.

We pray today for
loving parents for children.
We remember
those who no longer see dad or mum,
those abused,
those exploited
by people who should care for them.

Lord, in your mercy,
HEAR OUR PRAYER.

We pray today for
health for children.

We remember those in hospital,
those who are dying.
Surround them with your love
and the healing you alone can give.

Lord, in your mercy,
HEAR OUR PRAYER.

And we pray for ourselves
that the child within our spirit
be set free
to respond to life
with creative freedom.

Lord, in your mercy,
HEAR OUR PRAYER.

We bless you baby Jesus,
for coming among us,
playing beside us,
laughing with us.
Bless us all this Christmas.
AMEN

Chris Polhill

CHRISTMAS BAPTISMAL HYMN

(Tune: Infant lowly, infant holy)

Lord, we meet you,
Christ, we greet you,
born a child and yet a King.
Round your cradle,
in the stable,
we would each our praises bring.
From above us, you come near us,
show you love us, ever hear us.
Now to you we glory sing.
Now to you we glory sing.

Saviour Jesus,
now be near us
as we bring our lives to you.
In our children
may your love sing.
May they know your promise true.
Water flowing, Spirit sending,
faith a-growing, Love unending.
Take their lives and make them new.
Take their lives and make them new.

In their growing
keep them knowing
of the wonder of your love.
Root their living
in the giving
of the Saviour from above.
Living Jesus, stand among us;
ever with us, go before us.
In our lives your Spirit move.
Let us all your loving prove.

Leith Fisher

REMEMBERING WITH MARY
A service for the Sunday after Christmas

This service is based on four short meditations. The outline of each meditation is given and may be expanded upon by the leader – use reflections, poems … Four candles are set in a central position. After each meditation, a member of the congregation lights one of these candles to introduce a time of silent prayer, which is ended by an Amen or very brief prayer from the leader (e.g. 'Christ, in your mercy, hear our prayers').

Short prayer to open

First carol

Reading: Luke 2:19

Meditation:
Mary remembers: how it all began … the visit of the angel … people's reactions … Joseph's reaction … the marriage that almost didn't happen.

Reading: Matthew 1:18–25

A candle is lit.

Time of silent prayer for those who are finding life difficult; for those who feel misunderstood; for those whose marriages are under strain.

Second carol

Meditation:
Mary remembers: the long journey … the search for a place to stay…the innkeeper who welcomed them.

Reading: Hebrews 12:1–2,12–13

A candle is lit.

Silent prayer for our own spiritual journeys; for our own ministries of hospitality, that we may be more welcoming of people, more welcoming of Christ.

Third carol

Meditation:
Mary remembers: the visitors, shepherds, angels, wise men.

Readings: 1 John 1:1–3 and 1 Peter 1:10–12

A candle is lit.

Silent prayer for unexpected guests; for people who struggle with difficult questions.

Fourth carol

Meditation:
Mary remembers: the baby being born, her baby…God's son.

The final candle is lit.

Silent prayer – thanking God for Jesus Christ, our saviour.

Final carol

Blessing

Margaret Harvey

CHRISTMAS PLAYS

OH WHAT A NIGHT!

(A light-hearted version of the nativity, with serious intent. This has worked well with all ages, but depends on skilled and committed delivery. It can be used as a springboard for group discussion – the implications of nativity in a modern context …)

Characters:

Joseph	Helen
Mary	PJ
Stan	Crowd of revellers

Scene 1: On a street

Loud music is blaring; a few revellers/party animals stagger into view, perhaps covered in streamers, carrying beer cans. They start chanting the name of the local city/town, e.g. 'Manchester, Manchester, Manchester …' in a beery fashion, and fall about laughing. They stagger on a bit, then start singing the pop song 'Last Christmas I gave you my heart' in a suitably drunken manner. At this point, Mary and Joseph enter, the latter carrying a suitcase; both look haggard and harassed, Mary especially (which isn't surprising given the fact that she's heavily pregnant). One of the drunken revellers accidentally bumps into Mary, but seems to ignore her.

Joseph: Oi, watch it! She's pregnant.

The revellers seem to take no notice and move offstage.

Joseph: People today! Just got no manners. *(Joseph 'trawls' his throat, and 'gobs' on the pavement.)*

Mary: Oh, forget it. Let's just find somewhere to stay. And, Joseph, will you stop spitting in the street. It's disgusting.

Joseph pulls a face to indicate that he feels nagged. He stops suddenly when Mary turns to him and says:

Mary: Look, I think there are some hotels over there. Come on.

They head to a different part of the set. Mary and Joseph begin to mime knocking on doors, talking to hoteliers, negotiating a place to stay, and being constantly turned away. Mary becomes increasingly frustrated/angry; Joseph becomes more and more despondent/depressed. Finally, they sit down in the street. Mary's anger is fuelled by the pain she is beginning to feel.

Mary:	I just don't believe this. Everywhere's full, and when you ask 'why?', they just say, 'Don't you know it's Christmas?' Whatever that is. I mean, what with that and this damn census we'll never get anywhere. *(With real venom)* It's all your fault, this! Why couldn't you have been born somewhere closer to home? But, no, you have to be born a hundred miles from the nearest civilised town.
Joseph:	*(glumly)* Aw, [city/town] isn't that bad.
Mary:	And what's worse we could've got a room if that pathetic car of yours hadn't broken down five miles from town and left us to walk. Huh, car! I say 'car', if that's what you call a 1972 Ford Cortina with furry dice in the window –
Joseph:	It's a classic, that is.
Mary:	It's a pile of scrap. When the AA man turned up to fix it, he laughed, said, 'I'm not in the comedy business', and cleared off. And then, to cap it all, here I am like a beached whale.
Joseph:	You said it.
Mary:	What?
Joseph:	Nothing.
Mary:	So here I am stranded like a beached whale, ready to pop a sprog at any moment, with only the winner of 'Mr Waste of Space 200__' for company. It's about time you did something! *(Mary puts her head in her hands.)*
Joseph:	*(to the audience)* I know she thinks I'm a fool, but she doesn't know how much I love her. Or how scared I am. I just don't know what's going on. I mean, I know I'm not the father, despite what everyone says, but Mary says … Mary says the father's God. What kind of talk is that? I laughed at first – and more – but now I'm not so sure. You see, she's so sure, so confident … I don't know. I don't care much about this God thing. I just know I love her and I'll always be there for her. *(Joseph puts his head in his hands.)*
Mary:	*(to the audience)* I'm so scared. I know I shouldn't take it out on him, but I'm so scared. And he probably thinks I hate him, but I love him to the depth of myself. I'm just so confused. OK, I couldn't believe it at first – that God would give me a child. I didn't even want one. I mean, I'm still at school. I want a career. But when I got pregnant, I have to admit I felt a bit special. Well, it was amazing. God and me. Except no one seemed to

believe me or approve. But Joseph was there for me. But now I'm not sure about things. I mean, if I'm carrying God's child what am I doing on the streets? And at the rate we're going, that's where it's going to be born. How can God want that?

Mary and Joseph look at each other, speak each other's name lovingly, and then collapse into each other's arms; at which point, Mary starts to go into labour.

Mary: Oh my God, it's starting. Joseph, it's starting. It's starting … Joseph. Do something!

Joseph: Right, yes, right! Um … *(gets up in a fumbling manner; starts running up and down, talking to (imaginary) passersby, trying to elicit help).* Look, I wonder if you could … would you? … Oh … There's a pregnant woman here who needs help …… Why won't anyone help? Heeelllppp! *(No response; then, to Mary)* I know, I'll call an ambulance *(fumbles for his phone but can't find it).* Where's my phone? I can't find my phone. Damn, I bet it's still in the car. *(To passersby)* Can I borrow your phone? Please, please – damn it, why won't anyone help? *(To Mary)* Just wait here. I'll find a payphone, I'll be back in a minute.

Mary: *(in serious pain)* No, Joseph, no! Don't leave me … I'm scared … Oooh, I think it's coming … Just get me off the street.

Joseph begins to help Mary to her feet; at this point a scruffy and dirty-look-ing stranger (Stan) joins him to help.

Stan: Here, let me …

Mary: *(not fully aware of Stan's presence)* Yeugh, what's that smell?

Joseph: *(defensively)* I've done nothing!

Stan: Come on, let's get her off the street.

Mary: *(becoming aware of Stan)* Yeugh, who's this? God, is it a dosser? *(She has another contraction.)* Oh no, it's coming!

Stan: *(to Joseph)* Look, let's get her off the street. I've got a place down this alley. We'll sort her out from there.

Joseph: Well …

Stan:	We've no time to argue. Come on.

They help Mary offstage (behind some sort of screen). The rest of the dialogue in this scene is delivered offstage, from a microphone, if needed.

Joseph:	So where's your place, then?
Stan:	This is it.
Joseph:	I don't know how to tell you this, mate, but it's a cardboard box and some newspapers.
Stan:	It's all I've got.
Mary:	*(shouting in pained anger)* When you two have finally finished talking about home furnishings, could you get your butts down here and give me a hand? This thing is going to come out any minute.
Joseph:	Oh God, I think I'm going to faint.

Scene 2

The back alley of the previous scene is now centre stage. There is a cardboard box and papers strewn everywhere. Mary sits, exhausted but happy, against a wall, cradling her baby. The baby is wrapped up in someone's shirt. Joseph sits next to her, 'coochicooing'. Stan stands looking about him.

Stan:	*(to himself)* We should get the baby and mother to a hospital.

Joseph overhears this, gets shaken out of his doting, and stands in order to talk to Stan.

Joseph:	Look, I don't know how to thank you ... don't even know your name.
Stan:	Stan.
Joseph:	Er, Joseph ... *(They shake hands; then Joseph, visibly losing his reservations, hugs Stan.)* And this is my girlfriend ... my wife ... Mary ... Mary, this is Stan.
Mary:	Stan, what you did was wonderful ... And I'm so sorry about what I said, you know, about you being a dosser.

Stan shrugs.

Mary: Would you like to hold him?

Stan: Erm, no, I don't think I should …

Mary: Please, Stan, I couldn't think of anyone I'd trust more to hold him.

Stan: *(holding the baby)* What are you going to call him?

Mary: *(looking at Joseph as much as at Stan)* We're going to call him Jesus, Emmanuel.

Stan: Cool. A bit weird though.

Mary: It means 'God with us'.

Enter Helen, a prostitute.

Helen: Hey, Stan, what's happening? Have you been sowing your wild oats again?

Stan hastily passes the baby back to Mary.

Stan: Oh, Helen, you all right? I'm just helping out this lot.

Helen: So we heard. Your mate Reg saw the whole thing. It's the news on the street – you're a regular superhero. A few of us were wondering if we could help? Come on, Stan, aren't you going to introduce us?

Stan: Yeah, of course, Helen … Mary and Joseph and baby Jesus.

Helen: Cool name. Bit weird though.

Stan: Yes, yes, we've done that one already.

Helen crouches down beside Mary and Joseph.

Helen: *(to Mary)* Aw, isn't he gorgeous? … You're so lucky … Look, I know you don't know me, but if you need a nicer place to stay for a bit, you can come to mine. It gets a bit hectic, but it's warm.

Stan: *(sarcastically)* Is that the flat or the bed? Come on, Helen, a hooker's flat is hardly the place for a nice family.

Helen: And this is?

Stan:	And there's PJ to deal with.
Helen:	Look, he's all right. He'll be here in a minute.
Stan:	What do you want to go asking that useless smackhead over for?
Helen:	He's just bringing some things for the baby.
Mary:	Please, don't argue. You're both great. You've done loads already. But I think it would be wise if Jesus and I went to a hospital to get checked over. What do you think?
Helen:	Yeah, you're right.
Joseph:	That's what I was going to say. I'll go and ring for an ambulance.
Stan:	I'll come with you, if you don't mind.
Joseph:	Sure, come on. Back in a tic. *(Joseph kisses Mary.)*
Helen:	You've got a good bloke there.
Mary:	He has his uses!
Helen:	Look, I brought a few things. I thought you might need them.
	Helen takes a blanket out of a carrier bag.
Mary:	That's lovely.
Helen:	And I found some wipes and a towel, oh, and this perfume stuff. You know, if you or baby need to get cleaned up, like. And the smelly stuff is fine for Jesus. It's hypo-allergenic. I checked.
Mary:	Thank you. I don't know what to say. We don't deserve all this.
Helen:	Don't be silly. It's nothing.
Mary:	You're wrong. It's everything.
	Pause
	Joseph and Stan re-enter.
Joseph:	All done. The ambulance will be here as soon as it gets through the traffic *(goes over to Mary and sits down beside her)*.

PJ enters.

Stan: Well, look who it isn't!

PJ: Pleasure to see you too, Stan.

Helen: PJ, you got here. Come and meet everyone – Mary, Joseph and the little 'un, Jesus.

PJ: Cool name, bit weird though.

Helen: Yes, yes … Did you get the things I asked for?

PJ: Yeah, nicked 'em from the late-night Boots.

Helen: Oh, PJ!

PJ: Well, old habits and all that. I got nappies and dummies and everything. I'm a walkin' maternity ward.

Helen: Well, thanks anyway. *(To Mary)* His heart's in the right place.

Mary: *(to PJ)* Would you like a look at Jesus?

PJ: Oh, could I? Never really been near a baby before. *(Looks in; starts coochicooing.)*

Mary: PJ's an unusual name. What does it stand for?

PJ: Psycho Jack. But my friends just call me Psycho.

Mary: Lovely … *(Thinks for a second)*. You could hold him if you like.

PJ: Aw, could I?

Helen: Now, be careful.

           Stan comes and joins the adoration scene.

Helen: You two have got someone really special there.

Stan & PJ: *(together, agreeing)* Yeah.

Mary: It's going to sound stupid, but I think we all have, like, 'cos we're all part of his family too …

Silence

Stan: *(turns)* Look, there's some flashing lights. Come on, it's the ambulance. Let's get you into the warm.

Epilogue

Stan, Helen and PJ in line facing the congregation/audience.

Stan: I never thought I mattered.

Helen: They called me a tart and a waste of space.

PJ: I was labelled a menace to society … Come to think of it, I *am* a menace to society.

All: But tonight was different.

Stan: Because I wasn't ignored.

Helen: Because I wasn't just being used by someone else.

PJ: Because someone let *me* help.

All: Tonight was different.

Stan: Tonight I counted.

Helen: Tonight I was accepted for who I am.

PJ: Tonight I didn't have to play the thug.

All: Because of a child.
           Because it was OK to show love,
           to be vulnerable and real,
           to see the world in a new way,
           to be loved.
           If there is a God, tonight he has been among us.

Rachel Mann

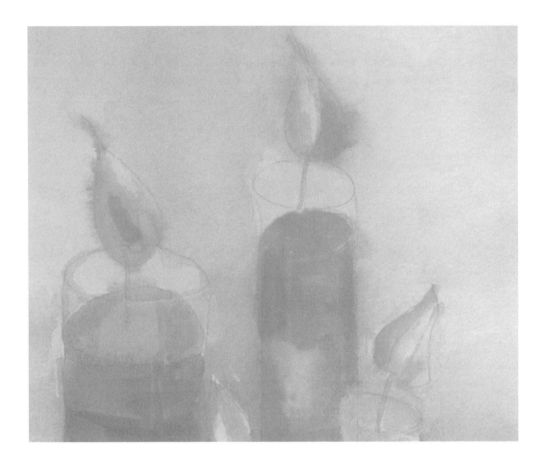

THE SHEPHERDS' PLAY

Characters:

Two narrators, or one will do
Several lambs (optional) – small children could play these parts
Three shepherds
Thief
Three angels
Mary
Joseph

Costumes:

The shepherds, angels and Mary and Joseph are traditionally dressed. The narrators could wear black trousers and white tops with Christmasy flowers in their buttonholes. The thief is in black and wears a mask.

Props, etc:

For narrators	– *several toy lambs, unless the parts of lambs are taken by children, in which case only one toy lamb will be needed.*
For shepherds	– *tripod and cooking pot, ladle, three bowls, three spoons*
	– *crooks (not essential, but generally associated with shepherds)*
	– *blankets (not essential)*
	– *imitation fire (placed somewhere hidden, e.g. behind a screen or pillar.)*
For thief	– *a sack marked 'SWAG'*
For angels	– *a knuckle-duster (brass knuckles)*
For Mary and Joseph	– *a manger/crib*
	– *a stool*
	– *a doll to represent baby Jesus*

Other hymns and carols that could be used:

Away in a manger
Come and sing the Christmas story
In the bleak midwinter
Silent night

(Enter two narrators from the back of the church. They are carrying several woolly, toy lambs, which they place strategically around the church. Alternatively, they are accompanied by small children dressed as lambs. If the latter, then the narrators shepherd them to various places. The children could be encouraged to 'baa' and play up as required. Having sorted the lambs out, the narrators then take up their positions to one side of the acting area and speak the following.)

Narrators 1 & 2:	Long ago and far away,
	Yet here, and close to hand,
	Three shepherds watching through the night,
	A sad, forsaken band.
	Frozen cold, in icy dark,
	They wait for time to pass,
	And hope to see the coming dawn,
	When light will come at last.

(During this speech, the three shepherds progress through the congregation. They all look very fed up. Shepherds one and two are shivering, blowing on their fingers, wrapping their arms around themselves ... Shepherd three is staggering under the weight and awkwardness of the tripod and pot, three bowls and spoons, ladle, crooks and blankets. Shepherd one is bullying him and pushing him around. Shepherd three is allowing himself to be thoroughly cowed and intimidated and keeps falling over, dropping things and generally dithering around. The shepherds reach the centre of the acting area.)

Shepherd 1:   *(fed up)* I'm cold.

Shepherd 2:   *(ordering Shepherd three)* You! Go and light a fire!

Shepherd three tries to do just that. The other two watch him critically, drumming their fingers impatiently and raising their eyes to heaven as he fumbles around. Having fiddled ineffectually for a few moments, whittling sticks or whatever, Shepherd three suddenly triumphantly produces the (artificial) fire. This should amuse the audience, but Shepherds one and two remain unmoved.

Shepherd 1:   *(continuing to moan)* I'm hungry.

Shepherd 2:   *(to Shepherd three, as before)* Heat up some stew!

Shepherd three fetches the tripod and the cooking pot, which he places over the fire.

Shepherd 1:   *(aggressively)* And I don't want lamb again!

Shepherd 2:   *(bullying)* Go on ... stir it ... serve it!

Shepherd three does so.

Shepherd 1:   *(tasting it with disgust)* It *is* lamb. Again.

Shepherd 2:   *(riled)* Well, what do you expect around here? Fish and chips?

Shepherd 1:   *(still moaning)* And I'm tired too.

Shepherd 2:   *(thoroughly fed up with him)* Well, go to sleep then.

Shepherd 1:   *(indignantly)* How am I supposed to sleep? This is a dangerous place. There are wolves and bears everywhere!

Shepherd 2:   *(to Shepherd three)* You! Go and keep watch! *(Shepherd three takes up a position in the acting area as if standing guard.)* I'm going to sleep now. *(Shepherd two settles down beside the fire.)*

Shepherd 1:   *(sticking to his guns)* And there are thieves around as well, you know.

Shepherd two gives an exaggerated snore.

Shepherd 1:   *(Realising no one's listening)* Hmph. Never wanted to be a shepherd anyway. *(He also settles down to sleep.)*

Shepherds one and two both snore noisily for a few moments. Then, suddenly, up pops the thief from somewhere in the congregation. He sings:

Thief's song

Words and music: Alison Pearson

(The thief starts to creep through the audience, looking over his shoulder and tiptoeing in an exaggerated way. He is carrying his sack marked 'SWAG'. He comes up to Shepherd three, who by now is falling asleep on his feet.)

Thief:	I spy with my little eye someone who's really no good. Stupid and sleepy and gets pushed around. *(The thief gives Shepherd three a shove. Shepherd three jumps but doesn't really know what's going on.)* He stands between me and my food!

The thief begins to creep round Shepherd three towards a nearby lamb.

Shepherd 3:	*(half coming round)* Whassat?
Thief:	*(flaps arms like wings)* Too whit, too woo.

Shepherd three is reassured. The thief creeps nearer the lamb. Shepherd three starts, and looks in his direction.

Thief:	Baa, baa!

This time Shepherd three is not so convinced. He walks over to investigate, and trips over the thief.

Thief:	*(slightly hysterically)* I'm a rock, I'm a rock!
Shepherd 3:	*(convinced, hopping around on one foot)* Ouch! Ouch, blooming rock!

Shepherd three hops back to his guard post. The thief watches him and, when he is sure that he's dropping asleep again, creeps towards a toy lamb and stuffs it into his sack.

Thief:	Got it! *(He starts to creep away.)*

Angels' song
(Sung to the tune of Ding Dong Merrily On High)

As the angels start singing, the thief falls to the ground in a terrified heap. The shepherds leap to their feet and freeze, equally amazed.

Listen shepherds, don't be scared,
Good News to you we're bringing;
A child is born in Bethlehem,
and you must go and greet him:
Gloria, Hosanna in excelsis

Glory be to God on high,
peace and goodwill are given,
to all people on the earth,
to bring them close to heaven:
Gloria, Hosanna in excelsis

The angels flutter into the background. The shepherds look at one another in wonder.

Shepherd 2:   *(stage whisper to Shepherd one)* Can you see what I can see?

Shepherd 1:   *(dumbfounded)* Er … yes.

Shepherd 2:   *(to the thief)* Can you see what I can see? *(He does a double take.)* Who are you?

Thief: I'm – er – Peter. I'm just – er – keeping one of your lambs warm. *(He takes the lamb out of his sack and sets it back on the ground.)* There's a nice lamb!

Shepherd 2:   *(to Shepherd three)* Can *you* see what I can see?

Shepherd 3:   Er … yes. *(Suddenly finding his assertive self)* And I think we ought to do what they say. *(He has surprised himself. The other two shepherds look at him in amazement.)*

Shepherd 1:   *(highly indignant)* I beg your pardon!

Shepherd 3:   *(trembling in his sandals)* I said, I think we should do what these good people *(the angels take offence)* – er – angels, say, and go to Bethlehem and find this baby who is the Saviour, because *(heartfelt)*, frankly, some of us could do with a bit of saving; and, personally, I wouldn't mind a bit of peace and goodwill! *(This last is directed, forcefully, at Shepherds one and two.)*

Shepherd 2:   *(outraged)* Well really, I'm absolutely appalled at your behaviour! *(He advances on Shepherd three wagging his finger.)* Why I've a good mind to –

One of the angels comes and stands silently beside Shepherd three in support. Shepherd two thinks again and backs off.

Shepherd 1:   *(thinking he'll have a go)* If you think I'm walking all the way to Bethlehem, in the middle of the night, just to see a blooming baby, you've got another think coming.

Another angel advances on Shepherd one. He is wearing a knuckle-duster.

Angel: *(brandishing his fist)* Wanna knuckle sandwich, mate?

Shepherd one falls back in alarm. The angel places himself, somewhat menacingly, on the other side of Shepherd three. During this inter-action, the thief has started to tiptoe away.

Remaining angel: Oy, Sonny Jim, where do you think you're going? *(The thief freezes in mid-step, realises he can't escape, and is brought forcefully by the remaining angel to stand with Shepherds one and two.)*

Shepherd 3:   *(rather timidly but still up for it)* I – um – think we should *all* be – er – going now – as it were – um – to Bethlehem.

Shepherds one and two appear still doubtful. The three angels glance significantly at one another, then grab Shepherds one and two and march them off towards Bethlehem.

Shepherd 3:   *(to the audience)* I *think* they said peace and goodwill.

They all exit, Shepherd three taking the props with him.

Two of the angels bring on the manger/crib and a stool; exit. Mary and Joseph enter. Mary places the baby in the manger and sits down on the stool, with Joseph standing behind her. Music: introduction to 'Infant Holy' or 'Child in the Manger'. There is a knock at the door.

Joseph: Come in. We've been expecting you.

The angels, shepherds and thief enter and group themselves around the crib. Gradually, they take up attitudes of adoration and reverence.

Mary: I think this baby may make quite a difference to you.

Song: Infant Holy *or* Child in the manger *(sung by the angels, shepherds and thief)*

Shepherd 1:   Well, perhaps I could stop being so grumpy.

Shepherd 2:   And perhaps I could stop ordering people around so much.

Shepherd 3:   And perhaps I could stop letting myself be pushed around.

Thief: Perhaps I could stop taking things that don't belong to me.

Shepherd 1:   In fact – I could start being happy.

Shepherd 2:   And I could start doing things for myself.

Shepherd 3:   And I could stand up for myself.

Thief: And I could be content with what I have. *(He turns impulsively to Shepherd one.)* I'm sorry I took your lamb. It was only because I was so *(playing to the gallery)* hungry!

Shepherd 1:   My dear chap, why on earth didn't you say so. Just come with me, I've got some wonderful lamb stew made by my good friend *(indicating Shepherd three)* over here. He'll get you some. *(He suddenly thinks better of it.)* Ah, no, on second thought, I'll get it for you myself. In fact, I'll get us all some. Come on.

                  Slapping the thief jovially on the back and linking arms with Shepherds two and three, he escorts them all out through the middle of the congregation.

Mary: Yes, I think this baby is going to make quite a difference.

Narrators: Long ago and far away,
                  Yet here and close to see,
                  Our shepherds now have found the babe,
                  Their Saviour, Christ to be.
                  Warmed in heart, content in soul,
                  They walk their pathway fast,
                  For now they see that dawn is here,
                  And light has come at last.

                  Music

Alison Pearson

WOW! GOOD NEWS

A play for church or elsewhere. Use the space you have creatively.

Characters:

Parent	*Innkeeper 3*
Child/Children	*Shepherds*
Father Christmas	*Sheep*
Mary	*Angel*
Angel	*King*
Joseph	*Wise man 1*
Emperor	*Wise man 2*
Soldiers	*Wise man 3*
Innkeeper 1	*Wise man 4*
Innkeeper 2	

Prop:
A star dangling from a long stick

Setting:
A family home at Christmastime.

Parents arguing, children arguing: 'Mine, mine, mine, mine!'

Parent:	*(exasperated)* Christmas, Christmas, Christmas. What is Christmas for anyway?! Who needs it?!

Big flash or other effect. Father Christmas emerges from under the church organ.

Father Christmas:	You need Christmas. It's good news. I am Father Christmas.
Child:	Can we call you Santa?
Father Christmas:	All right. You can call me many other things too: Père Noël, Nikolaus, Knecht Ruprecht. The Christmas Man. Sometimes I wear red, sometimes I wear black or green. I am always old, and often merry.
Child:	Presents, presents, presents, presents …
Father Christmas:	Sometimes I am frightening, sometimes I am kind. What you call me depends on who you are.
Child:	Presents, presents, presents, presents …
Father Christmas:	But whatever you call me, I have a story to tell you which is much more important.
Child:	Presents, presents, presents, presents …
Father Christmas:	But the story is even more important than the presents.
Child:	Wow.
Father Christmas:	The story is better than presents because every time folk listen to this story, the world becomes a better place.
Child:	Wow.
Father Christmas:	And looking at this house tonight, I think I'd better tell it right now. Call me Santa, call me Father Christmas, but now I am the story-teller, so you'd better listen.
Child:	Wow.

☆ ☆ ☆

Father Christmas:	Let's tell the story. Scene one: A wee town called Nazareth.

Necessary players troop in.

Mary:	I am Mary. I am young. I am not married. I live at home.

Big flash or other effect

Angel:	I am the angel Gabriel. I am God's messenger. Thundercrash and lightning. Very, very frightening.
Mary:	Wow. I am Mary. I am young. I am not married. I *am* frightened.
Angel:	Mary, God thinks you are great. You are going to have a baby.
Mary:	I am Mary. I am young. I am not married. I am frightened.
Angel:	Yes, yes. God will look after all that. But you will have a baby.
Mary:	I am young. I am not married. I am going to have a baby. Wow.

Players troop out.

☆ ☆ ☆

Father Christmas:	Scene two: Joseph finds out.

Necessary players troop in.

Joseph:	I am Joseph. I am a carpenter. I am a good man. I am going to marry Mary.

Big flash or other effect

Angel:	I am the angel Gabriel. I am God's messenger. Thundercrash and lightning. Very, very frightening.
Joseph:	Wow. I am Joseph. I am a carpenter. I am frightened.
Angel:	Mary will have a baby.
Joseph:	I am a good man. Does that mean I can't marry her?
Angel:	Don't be afraid. God will look after all that.
Joseph:	All right.

Players troop out.

☆ ☆ ☆

Father Christmas: Scene three: Rome

Necessary players troop in. This scene is acted up in the church pulpit.

Emperor: I am the emperor, I am very important and very rich.
    But I want to be even richer.

Soldiers: Yes, your majesty. Very good, your majesty.

Emperor: Go and count everyone to make sure I get my taxes.
    Just get it done.
    I don't mind if it's inconvenient. I am the emperor,
    I am very important and very rich.

Soldiers: Yes, your majesty. Very good, your majesty.

    Players troop out.

☆ ☆ ☆

Father Christmas: Scene four: Close to Bethlehem

    Necessary players troop in.

Mary: I am young. I am going to have a baby. I am getting fed up.

Joseph: I am Joseph. I am good. My family came from here. We have walked eighty miles. I am tired.

Mary: I am very tired.

Innkeeper 1:   No room here.

Mary: I am young. I am tired. I am going to have a baby.

Innkeeper 1:   No room here.

Mary: I am young. I am tired. I am going to have a baby.

Innkeeper 2:   No room here.

Mary: I am young. I am tired. I am going to have a baby.

Innkeeper 3:   No room here.

Mary: Please!

Innkeeper 3:   In the stable!

Joseph:	All right!

Players troop out.

☆ ☆ ☆

Father Christmas:	Scene five: On the hills nearby

Necessary players troop in

Shepherds:	We are shepherds. Nobody likes us.
Sheep:	We are sheep. Baa.

Big flash or other effect

Angel:	I am the angel Gabriel. I am God's messenger. Thundercrash and lightning. Very, very frightening.
Shepherds:	Wow. We are shepherds. We are frightened.
Sheep:	We are sheep. We are frightened too. Baa. Wow. Baa.
Angel:	I bring good news. Your King is born today. The King everyone has been waiting for. And he wants to see you.
Shepherds:	We are shepherds. Nobody likes us.
Sheep:	We are sheep. Baa.
Angel:	God likes you. And you will find your King dressed in baby clothes, lying in a manger. Leave the sheep and get down there.
Sheep:	Baa.
Father Christmas:	Suddenly there were lots of angels, all praising God.

Big flash or other effect

Angel:	(sing) Glory to God, glory to God, glory in the highest. To God be glory for ever. Alleluia. Amen.
Sheep:	Baa.

Players troop out.

☆ ☆ ☆

Father Christmas:	Scene six: The stable in Bethlehem
	Necessary players troop in.
Mary:	I am Mary. I am a mother. I have just given birth. I am glad that is over with.
Joseph:	I am Joseph. I am good. I am glad it is over with too.
Shepherds:	We are shepherds. Nobody likes us.
Mary:	I like you.
Joseph:	So do I.
Mary:	And so does Jesus.
Shepherds:	Baby clothes. Manger. The King. Hooray! Glory to God, glory to God, glory in the highest. To God be glory for ever. Alleluia. Amen.
	The angels enter, and raise the star .
	Players troop out.

☆ ☆ ☆

Father Christmas:	Scene seven: Herod's Palace
	Necessary players troop in. This scene is acted up in the pulpit.
King:	I am the king, I am very important. And I will kill anyone who says I am not.
Soldiers:	Yes, your majesty. Very good, your majesty.
Wise man 1:	We are wise men.
Wise man 2:	We are wise.
Wise man 3:	We followed a star.
Wise man 4 (or 1):	We have brought presents for the King.
King:	Presents, presents, presents, presents … I am the king, I am very important. And I will kill anyone who says I am not.

Wise man 1:	You are not the King.
King:	Soldiers!
Soldiers:	Yes, your majesty. Very good, your majesty.
Wise man 2:	Not the King we are looking for.
King:	Soldiers!
Soldiers:	Yes, your majesty. Very good, your majesty.
Wise man 3:	Our King is a baby.
King:	Tell me where he is. So I can give him presents too.
Wise man 4 (or 1):	We don't know yet. Goodbye. *(They leave.)*
King:	Find out where they go. And kill all the babies. I am the king.
Soldiers:	Yes, your majesty. Very good, your majesty.
	Players troop out.

☆ ☆ ☆

Father Christmas:	Scene eight: A house in Bethlehem
	Necessary players troop in.
Mary:	I am happy. Jesus is my baby.
Joseph:	I have found work. We will live here for now.
Wise man 1:	We are wise men.
Wise man 2:	We are wise.
Wise man 3:	We followed a star.
Wise man 4 (or 1):	We have brought presents for the King.

Wise man 1:	Gold for the King.
Wise man 2:	Frankincense for prayer.
Wise man 3:	Myrrh to ease pain.
Mary:	Oh, thank you.
Wise man 4 (or 1):	Watch out for the other king.
Joseph:	I've had a dream. The angel said …

Big flash or other effect

Angel:	Get out now.
Mary:	We'd better leave.
Wise man 2:	So had we.
Father Christmas:	Mary and Joseph and the baby Jesus went to Egypt until the old king had died. They were refugees. They had no home of their own. But God kept them safe. Because Jesus is the King who will change the world. More important than the emperor with all his riches. More important than the king with his soldiers. More important than the presents we give to remind ourselves about him. Jesus is the King who loves us.
Shepherds:	We are shepherds. Nobody likes us.
Father Christmas:	Jesus is the King who loves us all. Whoever we are. That's good news! I will see you late Christmas Eve, after I have been to church. Be good now!

Big flash or other effect; he leaves.

David Coleman

ANGELS, INC:

A mystery play based on the gospels of Matthew and Luke

A play for church or elsewhere. Use the space you have creatively.

Characters:

Angel (narrator)	*Joseph*
Angels	*Shepherd 1*
Gabriel	*Shepherds*
Elizabeth	*Angel 1*
Zechariah	*Wise men*
Mary	*Herod*

Prop:
A star dangling from a long stick

Scene 1: Angels, Inc

Angel (narrator):   Angels, they are messengers.
They have a job to do.
Bright they appear with word and flame
to get God's message through.

        Angels sit around a table with their feet up. A sign hangs on wall 'Angels, Inc: We get through!' Gabriel is asleep. The others are playing cards. (This carries on for a longer time than the audience expects.) A telephone rings; Gabriel remains asleep. The others poke him.

Gabriel: Eh, what.

Angel (narrator):   God's up to something … It's for you, Gabriel.

Gabriel: You what?

Angel (narrator):   Pick it up and find out. God's up to something.

Gabriel: *(answering the phone)* Hello, Angels Incorporated. We get the message through. Fire, brimstone, portents, dreams. How can we help you? *(Listening)* …Yes, an old man called Zechariah … How old? And his wife, Elizabeth. Going to have a baby?… How old? … Look, I am the angel Gabriel – certified Big and Terrifying and Powerful as they come. I put the fear of God into sinners. I am not here to mither pensioners. Couldn't you get some minor seraph for this one? *(Listening)* … Sor- ry! …You want me to go to the temple? Oh well, that's different. Great location, the temple. Nice and scary. *(Listening)* And Zechariah's on shift at the temple today. Burning incense, making smoke for prayers. OK, I know how to handle this. Message as good as sent!

Angel (narrator):   When Herod was King of Judea, there was a priest called Zechariah and his wife, Elizabeth. Both of them were good people. But they had no children. And they were getting on a bit.

Scene 2: The temple

Elizabeth: *(from offstage)* Zechari-ah! Zechari-ah!

Zechariah: All right, Lizzie. I know it's time I was up. I know I have work to do.

Elizabeth:	Zechari-ah!
Zechariah:	Oh, ar, um, yes, incense. Holy smoke, in fact. Here we go. *(He coughs, potters around.)*

Scene 3: The temple

Gabriel enters with a flourish. Zechariah sniffs the smoke, looks at the angel Gabriel, looks at the incense packet, looks at audience, carries on pottering.

Gabriel:	Zechariah!
Zechariah:	*(doesn't look up)* Eh what? Yes, that's me, Zechariah.
Gabriel:	Be not afraid!
Zechariah:	Do you think you could speak up, lad?
Gabriel:	Be not ... Look, I have a message for you. *(He unfurls a scroll and reads.)* Your wife, Elizabeth, will have a son, and you must name him John. John will be filled with the Holy Spirit and will lead many people back to God. But first, Elizabeth must give birth.
Zechariah:	What, old Lizzie have a son?
Gabriel:	I am an angel. What did you think I meant by 'have a son'?

There is a long pause.

Zechariah:	Lizzie have a son? ... Nah! *(He goes back to pottering.)*
Gabriel:	Look here, you old fool. I am Gabriel, as Big and Terrifying and Powerful as angels come. You have not believed a word I've said. So you won't speak a word – until it all comes true. *(He 'gags' Zechariah with a sticking plaster.)*
Elizabeth:	*(from offstage)* Zechari-ah!
Zechariah:	Mm mm mm ...

Exit Zechariah, enter Mary.

Angel (narrator):	One month later: In the village of Nazareth in Galilee. A girl called Mary.

Mary:	*(showing off her ring)* Nice ring, isn't it? Joseph Davidson gave it me. You know Joseph, the carpenter. We're getting married, you know.
	Gabriel appears, dramatically.
Mary:	Wow!
Gabriel:	Mary, God is pleased with you.
Mary:	Who, me? I didn't do it, really, I didn't.
Gabriel:	Oh give me strength! Look, Mary, sit down – have a cup of tea. And listen! Don't be afraid! – you got that – don't be afraid! *(Reads from the scroll)* God is pleased with you, Mary, and you are going to have a baby. His name will be Jesus. He will be great and will be called the Son of God. He will rule God's own people for ever, and his kingdom will never end.
Mary:	Hold on a minute, I've only just got engaged to Joseph Davidson. See, here's the ring. What's all this about having a baby?
Gabriel:	*(reads)* The power of God's Holy Spirit will come over you. So your baby will be called the holy Son of God and, and … *(pause).* Mary, you're just not following me, are you?
	Mary shakes her head, looks blank, frightened. The angel gives up, tosses away the scroll, and tries another tack.
Gabriel:	Look, you know old Lizzie?
Mary:	Yes.
Gabriel:	She's expecting.
Mary:	What?!
Gabriel:	You saw her going into the health centre last week? Antenatal classes. Just remember: Nothing is impossible for God! *Nothing* is impossible for God.
Mary:	OK, if you say so.
Gabriel:	You got that, nothing is impossible for God. God is God is God!
Mary:	OK.

Pause

Gabriel: You got that? Nothing is impossible for God, God is God. Nothing is impossible.

Other angels enter and gently lead Gabriel away.

Angel (narrator):   Look Gabriel, it's all right, she said yes. She said yes! Come on.

Mary: *(after all the angels have gone)* Help! What am I going to tell Joseph? What am I going to tell Joseph?

Joseph enters.

Mary: Joseph. I'm pregnant.

Joseph: Really?! Right, the wedding's off! You can keep the ring!

Mary: Oh no! *(runs off)*

Angel (narrator):   So Mary ran off. She ran off to see Lizzie. Off to the hills, to find God had been busy. Meanwhile, back in Nazareth:

Gabriel: Joseph!

Joseph: Help! Help!

Gabriel: Just stop that a minute will you! Now then. You love Mary, don't you?

Joseph: Yes.

Gabriel: And you don't really want to throw her out, do you?

Joseph: No, but she said she was pregnant and –

Gabriel: *(grabs hold of him and shakes him)* Joseph, listen to me: the baby that Mary will have is from the Holy Spirit. What God does is right, whatever anyone else might think. So you just go ahead and marry her. Then, after her baby is born, name him Jesus – because he will save his people from the things they do wrong. And nothing is impossible for God. Do you hear me? Nothing is impossible for God.

Angel (narrator):   Up in the hills, Mary reached her cousin's house.

Mary: *(at the church lectern)* Hello there! Lizzie? Anyone in?

Angel (narrator):	When Elizabeth heard Mary, God's Holy Spirit came upon Elizabeth. Then, in a loud voice, she said to Mary:

God has blessed you more than any other woman.
He has also blessed the child you will have.
How wonderful that the mother of my Lord should run away to me.

Angel (narrator):	And Mary sang this song:
Mary:	With all my heart, I praise the Lord,
and I am glad: God cares for me.

He drags tyrants from their thrones
and lifts us up, the lowly.
God gives the hungry tasty food;
the rich, they are left with nothing.

Interlude with Christmas carols (optional)

Angel (narrator):	Mary stayed with Elizabeth for three months. Then she went back home, just before Lizzie's baby was due.

Cries of a newborn baby. Enter Zechariah carrying the baby (this could be a doll). Zechariah waves the baby's hands, praising God. Angel 1 appears and removes the sticking plaster from Zechariah's mouth.

Zechariah:	Mm mm mm *(until his mouth is freed).*

Praise the Lord,
the God of Israel!
God has kept his promise.
You, my son, will be called
a prophet of God most high.
You will go before the Lord
to prepare his way.
You will show folk they are saved,
for sins can be forgiven.

Narrator:	At that time, the emperor ordered a census because he wanted to raise taxes. Everyone had to be registered in his hometown. So Joseph left Galilee and set off for Bethlehem, where his ancestors had been born.

Mary went with him to Bethlehem. And while they were there, her first baby was born. They dressed him in baby clothes. He slept in a manger, because there was no room for people like them.

Interlude with carols (optional)

Angel (narrator): That night in the fields near Bethlehem shepherds were guarding their sheep.

The angels, whispering, creep up and surround the shepherds.

Angels: Don't be afraid. Don't be afraid. Don't be afraid.

Shepherd 1: What was that?

Angel (narrator): Don't be afraid.

Shepherd 1: Help!

Gabriel: Oh for goodness' sake – don't be afraid! All right, boys, let 'em have it.

Angels: Glory to God, glory to God,
Glory in the highest.
To God be glory for ever.
Alleluia. Amen.

Gabriel: Now hear this: I have good news for you, which will make everyone happy. This very day, in King David's hometown, a saviour was born for you. He is Christ the Lord. You will find him in a stable, dressed in baby clothes, lying on a bed of hay.

Angels: Praise God in heaven!
Peace on Earth to everyone who pleases God.

The angels lead the shepherds to the manger.

Angel (narrator): When the shepherds saw Jesus, they told his parents what the angel had said about him. Everyone listened and was surprised. Meanwhile:

Gabriel: Have you got the star? Makes a change from just frightening people.

Angel 1: OK. *(He takes the star on the long stick and dangles it over the wise men, who follow it until they are face-to-face with Herod.)*

Angel (narrator):	Not far away, Herod was king in Jerusalem. And he wasn't pleased. Wasn't pleased in the least, when wise men from the east came and said:
Wise men:	Where is the child born to be King of the Jews? We saw his star rise and have come to worship him.
Angel (narrator):	Herod was even less pleased when the clever people of Jerusalem looked in holy books and found this:

God's promised King
will be born in Bethlehem.
A far greater town than you had ever thought,
because out of that town
there will come forth a leader,
a shepherd, a King,
for the people of God.

Herod:	Find him, then tell me. I'll send him a present. Off you go, don't be long. I look forward to hearing from you.
Angel (narrator):	They didn't have to go much further till they found the baby, and offered him the gifts that they'd brought for a King. *(The wise men offer their gifts. Then turn to go back.)*
Angel 1:	Hold on. You're not going back to Herod, are you? Oh no you don't. Off you go – the other way. Joseph! Wake up. Yes, it's us again. Never mind all that frightening stuff. There are worse things now than angels to be frightened about. It's not safe to stay here. Egypt's that way. Take Mary, take the baby and get out now. Soldiers are coming!
	Sounds: Tramp tramp tramp tramp. Soldiers with 'swords' come in and brutally stab the manger, run it through, 'shoot' at it, etc.
Angel (narrator):	Herod had sent soldiers to kill all the baby boys in Bethlehem.
Herod:	That'll teach them to listen to angels instead of the people in charge. *(Evil laugh).*
Mary:	With all my heart, I praise the Lord, and I am glad: God cares for me, God saves me.
	He shall drag tyrants from their thrones.

He shall lift up the lowly.
God shall give the hungry tasty food.
And those who will not share good things
will leave,
will leave with nothing.

Christmas carols

David Coleman

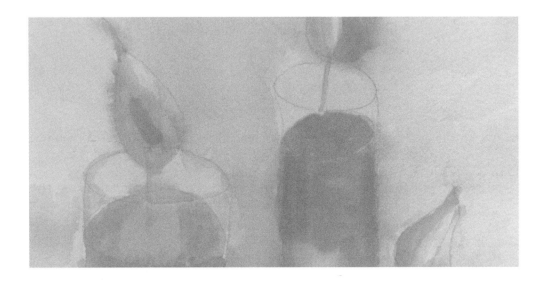

IS IT A KING?

Use the space you have creatively. Punctuate the play with Christmas carols if you wish.

Characters:
Four frightening, powerful angels
Ram, Nashon (soldiers in Herod's palace)
Mary
Joseph
Three speaking wise men (dressed as pretentious scientists) with any number of hangers-on.
One speaking shepherd, any number of other shepherds
Herod the Great
Hepzibah, a young woman of Bethlehem, Ram's girlfriend

Scene 1: The guard house, Herod's palace

Offstage voice:	Diiis-missed!

Enter Ram, a soldier

Ram yawns, lies down to sleep. From behind him come four frightening, powerful angels. They begin clapping rhythmically and, if possible, keep their claps on the bold type below. Ram remains sleeping.

Angel 1:	One, two, three, four …
All angels:	**Is** it a **king** you **rea**-lly **want**? **Is** it a **king** to **rule** you? **Is** it a **king** you **rea**-lly **want**?
Angel 1:	To **pile** up your **riches**.
Angel 2:	To **steal** your **children**.
Angel 3:	To **make** you **enemies**, **send** you **fighting**.
Angel 4:	**Give** up your **freedom**.
Angels 1 & 2:	*(voices fading)* And **fool** you and **fool** you and **fool** you and **fool** you and…
Angels 3 & 4:	**Is** it a **king** you **rea**-lly **want**? **Is** it a **king** to **rule** you? Or **do** you just **want** what a **king** ought to **bring**? Or **do** you just **want** what a **ruler** is **for**?
Angel 1:	**Justice** and **peace** and God's **love** ever**more**!
All angels:	One, two, three, four. Hey!

The angels vanish as quickly and spectacularly as possible.

Ram:	*(screams and sits up in bed)* My God! Help! Help! Oh my God!

These dreams! Must be that cheese sandwich I had on the last watch. If I were a superstitious man, I might think someone was trying to tell me something. As it is – well, just got to keep my nose clean, head down, keep the landlord happy. Smile and bow and scrape when the big nobs go by. Keep up the facade. Make sure the mask doesn't slip.

But then that's all *Herod* ever does anyway. Everyone knows he just muscled his way in here. Everyone knows he has no real right to call himself king. Everyone knows he's only where he is because of our enemies the Romans. But everyone knows what happens to anyone who lets on what everyone knows.

So, we all smile sweetly. Smile and bow and scrape. Keep up the façade. Maybe it's better the devil you know. At least you get your pay here. Helps you to look the other way. Let Herod get on with it.

Might get enough together soon to have a word with Hepzibah's dad down in Bethlehem. Can't wait to get back to her. My girl, Hepzibah. Says she *likes* a man in uniform … At least to start with! *(Chuckles)*.

No, can't wait … Just fed up with having to meet her in secret. We ought to move in together. That's the sort of dream I could really do with. *(Settles down again)* Hepzibah, Hepzibah, ahhh, Hepzibah! *(Snort/snore)*.

Scene 2: Nazareth

Joseph:	*(in bed, waking up)* … Mary … Mary … Ahh! Mary! Not long now. Not long now. What a lucky man I am.
	Knock. Enter Mary
Mary:	Joseph?
Joseph:	Yes, Mary, my love?
Mary:	I'm going to have a baby.
Joseph:	Oh my God!

Scene 3: The guard house, Herod's palace

Nashon: Bring another flagon of that stonking wine over here Ram!

Ram: OK, Nashon, good stuff this. Fit for a king!

Nashon: So it is, Ram, so it is, but old Herod won't miss a flagon or two – the amount he gets through! *(They laugh and drink.)* ... By the way, how did you end up with a name like *Ram*? Your mum fancy a shepherd or something?

Ram: Same way you ended up with *Nashon*. Ram was one of the king's ancestors. The *real* king, I mean, not this ... this ...

Nashon: I should watch your tongue, Ram!

Ram: Well, they say King Solomon had seven hundred *official* wives, *and* a few hundred more besides.

Nashon: Be difficult not to be a king's son! Maybe we're all king's sons.

Ram: I'm the king of the castle.

Nashon: Get down you dirty rascal.

Scene 4: Nazareth

All angels: **Is** it a **king** you **rea**-lly **want**?
                Is it a **king** to **rule** you?
                Or **do** you just **want** what a **king** ought to **bring**?
                Or **do** you just **want** what a **rul**er is **for**?
                Justice and **peace** and God's **love** ever**more**!
                Justice and **peace** and God's **love** ever**more**! *(voices fading)*

Joseph: Mary?

Mary: Yes, Joseph, my love?

Joseph: The good news or the bad news?

Mary: Go for the good first.

Joseph: It's all right. We will get married. God knows. I trust you. Let's make the most of what has happened.

Mary:	Oh Joseph. Thank God! And the bad news?
Joseph:	Mary, are you up to travelling? Because if you're sticking with me, we've got to go to Bethlehem. Emperor says so. And you're part of the royal family now, Mary. My dad always said he was in David's line. So it's Bethlehem we have to head for. Eighty miles in your condition. I'm sorry. Sure you still want to stay with me?
Mary:	What do you think, Joseph, my love? You're the best father on earth my son could have. *Our* son could have.
Joseph:	Our *son*?
Mary:	Oh, it *is* a son. I had a dream. I think.
Joseph:	*(pause)* So ... you had those dreams too?
Mary:	Yes. We'll call him Jesus.
Joseph:	It means 'God saves'. Let's hope so. Pray so.

Scene 5: The guard house, Herod's palace

Loud knocking

Ram:	Knock, knock, knock, who do you think you are?
Wise man 1:	Quite a deep question – but, for now, we just want to see the King.
Ram:	And which king might that be, pray?
Wise man 2:	*(confidently)* The one *our* research conclusively proves *must* be here.
Ram:	Oh, his nibs ... Sorry, I mean his serene majesty, King Herod. He won't see anyone until he's had his fill at the feast. Got some cracking dancers in tonight. Ducks off the pond! Phoarrr!
Wise man 3:	*(bemused)* Must be a feast to celebrate the birth .You know, Balthazar thought we should have brought a jewel-encrusted teddy bear, but I insisted on the gold, incense and myrrh. That's the proper protocol for baby kings, don't you know. Now just let us in, my good man; we've been working on this project for some while. And if we can show tangible results, we'll be able to renew the grant for our institute.

Wise man 1:	*(impatiently)* We've come a long way, from back east. Now, never mind this *Herod* character; where is the *baby* King. Star's in the sky. King must be here.
Ram:	Oh my God! *Somebody's* not going to like this!
All angels:	**Is** it a **king** you **rea**-lly **want?** **Is** it a **king** to **rule** you? Or **do** you just **want** what a **king** ought to **bring?** Or **do** you just **want** what a **ruler** is **for?** **Justice** and **peace** and God's **love** ever**more!** **Justice** and **peace** and God's **love** ever**more!** *(voices fading)*

Scene 6: Bethlehem, stable

Mary holds a swaddled baby.

Mary:	*(breathless)* Oh, Joseph. Oh my God.
Joseph:	*(almost equally breathless)* Oh, Mary. Oh my God.
Mary:	Isn't he beautiful? He is worth it all!
Joseph:	At least it's warm, here in this smelly old stable with the animals. And I suppose it's cheaper than the inn. You never know, I might be able to get work around here. Find somewhere to stay until you two are ready to move back.
First shepherd:	Is it all right to come in?
Joseph:	Who are you, why are you here?
First shepherd:	Where do we start? I think it must have been a dream, but we all had it. And we couldn't ignore it. And … and …
Joseph:	It's just possible that we know what you mean. I suppose you've come to see the baby.
First shepherd:	Come on in, lads, this is the place.

Shepherds come in and present gifts.

Angel 1:	One, two, three, four …

All angels:	**Is** it a **king** you **rea**-lly **want**? **Is** it a **king** to **rule** you? **Is** it a **king** you **rea**-lly **want**?
Angel 1:	To **pile** up your **riches**.
Angel 2:	To **steal** your **children**.
Angel 3:	To **make** you **enemies**, **send** you **fighting**.
Angel 4:	**Give** up your **freedom**.
Angels 1&2:	And **fool** you and **fool** you and **fool** you and **fool** you and … *(voices fading)*
Angels 3 & 4:	**Is** it a **king** you **rea**-lly **want**? **Is** it a **king** to **rule** you? Or **do** you just **want** what a **king** ought to **bring**? Or **do** you just **want** what a **ruler** is **for**?
Angel 1:	**Justice** and **peace** and God's **love** ever**more**!
All angels:	One, two, three, four. Hey!

Scene 7: The guard house, Herod's palace

Herod:	*(from as high up as possible, speaking very calmly and clearly, without any visible emotion, looking straight ahead)* Guards! *(claps twice).* *(Ram, Nashon and any others run to kneel before him.)* When those fools come back – follow them. *(Long pause)* But it looks like they took the road to Bethlehem. It's not far. *(Long pause)* I am the king. *(Pause)* It's hard being the king. *(Pause)* You have such responsibilities. Such heavy burdens. So much stress. Your hands are tied. *(Long pause)* I wouldn't want anyone to have to suffer as I do. All for the sake of my people. Got your swords?*(Long pause)* Bethlehem. *(Pause)* All the baby boys. Shall we say up to two years? Give or take *(draws his hand across his throat in a cutting gesture, makes a slitting noise). (Pause)* Off you go. *(He claps twice. Ram, Nashon and any others run out.)*
Angel 1:	One, two, three, four …
All angels:	**Is** it a **king** you **rea**-lly **want**?

Is it a **king** to **rule** you?
Is it a **king** you **rea**-lly **want**?

Angel 1:	To **pile** up your **riches**.
Angel 2:	To **kill** your **children**.
Angel 3:	To **make** you **enemies, send** you **fighting**.
Angel 4:	**Give** up your **freedom**.
Angels 1&2:	*(voices fading)* And **fool** you and **fool** you and **fool** you and **fool** you and …

Scene 8: A house in Bethlehem

Joseph:	Soldiers are coming. Mary, get the baby and run! *(They go to the door, which is suddenly blocked by Ram.)*
Ram:	Hold it right there. Give us the brat. Just doing my job.
Joseph:	Please. What if it were your own child?
Hepzibah:	*(comes running in, hugs Ram)* Ram!
Ram:	Hepzibah – get out! There's foul work to be done.
Hepzibah:	Ram, I'm going to have a baby. I'm going to have a baby.
Ram:	Oh my God! *(Ram puts his head in his hands; Joseph, Mary and Jesus hurry away.)*
Angel 1:	One, two, three, four …
All cast:	**Is** it a **king** you **rea**-lly **want**? **Is** it a **king** to **rule** you? **Is** it a **king** you **rea**-lly **want**? Or **maybe** the **Prince** of **Peace**?
	Silence

David Coleman

CHRISTMAS PLAY – WITH OR WITHOUT PUPPETS

Four actors (A, B, C, D) walk on and sit down in chairs facing the congregation/audience.

Actors remain deadpan and emotionless throughout the play, standing to say their lines then sitting down again.

Another idea, which works well, is to make wooden-spoon puppets to represent each character. Or the actors could wear different hats for different characters.

A: I am the narrator.

B: I am an actor.

C: I am an actor.

D: I am an actor.

A: This is a story about the first Christmas. It happened a long time ago. Mary and Joseph had to go to Bethlehem to be counted. They travelled on a donkey.

B: I'm Mary.

C: I'm Joseph.

D: I'm the donkey.

B: I'm pregnant.

C: I'm shocked.

D: I'm the donkey.

A: They arrived late and couldn't find anywhere to stay.

B: I'm tired.

C: I'm the innkeeper.

D: I'm the donkey.

C: We have nowhere for you to sleep.

B: My baby is due.

C: Oh dear. We only have a stable for your donkey.

D: I'm the donkey.

B: Perhaps we could sleep in your stable.

C: Yes, perhaps you could.

D: I'm the donkey.

A: Mary and Joseph and the donkey went to the stable. There were other animals there too.

B: I'm the ox – moo.

C: I'm the goat – baa.

D: I'm the donkey – eehaw.

A: Mary had the baby that night and laid him in a manger.

B: I'm Mary. This is my son.

C: I'm Joseph. I'm shocked.

D: I'm the manger. *(Stretches out arms. Mary reaches across and lays the 'baby', produced from under a chair, in D's arms.)*

A: In the fields nearby, there were some shepherds looking after their sheep.
B: I'm a shepherd.
C: I'm a sheep – baa.
D: I'm a donkey. *(All turn and look at D.)*
B: I'm a shepherd.
C: I'm a sheep – baa.
D: I'm a sheep – baa.

A: Suddenly they heard angels singing in the sky, telling of a saviour born in Bethlehem.
B: I'm a shepherd.
C: I'm an angel.
D: I'm a sheep – baa.
B: I'm afraid.
C: I'm singing.
D: I'm a sheep – baa.
A: The angels told the shepherds not to be afraid.
C: Don't be afraid.
B: All right, I won't.
D: Baa.

A: So the shepherds left their sheep.
D: Baa.
A: And went to find the stable. At the same time, or nearly, some wise men came from the East, following a star:
B: I'm a wise man.
C: I'm a wise man.
D: I'm a camel.
A: Their predictions told them that a great King was to be born and they followed the star to find his birthplace.
B: I have travelled many miles.
C: I have travelled many miles.
D: I'm a camel.
A: At first they called on King Herod, thinking that a great King must surely be born in a palace.
B: I'm a wise man.
C: I'm King Herod.
D: I'm a camel.
B: We seek a new baby who is to become a great King.
C: That's very interesting.
D: I'm a camel.

B:	Is he here?
C:	I don't think so.
B:	We'll have to search some more.
D:	I'm a camel.
C:	When you find him come and tell me. I want to worship him too.
B:	All right, I will.
D:	I'm the donkey. *(All turn and look at D.)* I'm the camel.
A:	At last they came to the stable and found the baby lying in a manger.
B:	We come to worship you.
C:	We come to bring you precious gifts.
D:	I'm a camel.
A:	The angels warned the wise men not to go back to King Herod.
B:	I'm a wise man.
C:	I'm an angel.
D:	I'm a camel.
C:	Don't go back to King Herod.
B:	All right, I won't.
D:	I'm a camel.
A:	And so the Saviour of the world was born on that first Christmas Day and the angels sang in the skies above.
B:	I'm an angel.
C:	I'm an angel.
D:	I'm *(long pause)* a donkey.
B:	Peace on earth.
C:	Goodwill to all people.
D:	And donkeys.
A:	The End.

All actors sit down, then stand up together and walk off.

Alix Brown

FOLLOW THE STAR!

A play/service for all ages

Characters:

The announcer – a young person, at the front by the microphone (small speaking role)

Minister – adult worship leader, at the front by the microphone (large speaking role)

The angel – in casual dress, e.g. white tracksuit and trainers (large speaking and singing role suitable for a very confident child, young person or adult). The angel may need a portable microphone. Prop needed: an alarm clock.

Young person A and Young person B – two young people or older children to help the angel. They are seated in the congregation (small speaking roles).

A group of shepherds – (suitable for a group of very young children; small speaking roles together in a group)

Star-holder with adult helper – sitting in the choir stall ready to go up to the lectern. For props they need a large glitter star and a torch/flashlight to illuminate the star in the dark (non-speaking roles).

People to make up the nativity scene – Mary, Joseph, babe, shepherds ... This scene could be completely inclusive, with children of all ages and adult helpers taking part. The nativity scene would probably be best set in the altar area of the church.

Any number of angels (who can be seated in the congregation)

Before the play/service:

The congregation will need service sheets titled 'Follow the Star!' and stars (lots of small ones). The stars could be made in a craft workshop before the service. On the service sheet include the congregational prayer said near the end of the play. The announcer opens the service – welcomes everyone, shows the crib, introduces the players.

Announcer:	Welcome everyone to our crib service here at _____ Church. We are glad you could come here tonight. The children from _____ are here *(points to the children by the crib)* to show you the Christmas story. And _____ *(minister)* is here to start the service with our first song.
Minister:	Thank you ... Getting ready for Christmas. Jobs to do. *(Here the minister names some jobs the minister does in the run-up to Christmas, e.g. school carol service – include local detail.)*
	As the minister is speaking, the angel (carrying an alarm clock) arrives and walks up the aisle noisily. The angel looks distracted and worried and interrupts the minister.
Angel:	Excuse me, is this a church? See, I've overslept and missed a meeting with Chief Angel Gabriel. Can you help me please? I've got a job to do but I don't know what, don't know where. But one of the other angels said, 'Ask at the church. They will help you.' Can I put my clock somewhere safe?
Minister:	Oh yes, put it up here out of the way. *(The angel sets the clock on the lectern.)*. Yes, I'll help you in a minute, but first I must start the service – it's a very busy time of year for a vicar, you know. *(The minister announces the first song.)*

Song: Little donkey

During the song the angel goes over to Young person A.

Angel:	*(at the end of the song)* Excuse me, but the vicar seems so busy with the service. Can you help me? See, I'm late and missed a meeting with Chief Angel Gabriel. Now I'm lost and don't know what I'm supposed to be doing.
Young person A:	Of course … The song might give us a clue. It's the Christmas story you are trying to help with, isn't it?
Angel:	Oh yes, didn't I say?
Young person A:	Well, in the song all the activity is about this mum and dad-to-be, Mary and Joseph, who have to go on a journey, just when their baby is due. So, that's the start. But do you think you could help me now with one of these songs? I've got to do it with the people for the service, but, really, I've been too busy getting ready for Christmas to practise!
Angel:	Oh, I like singing! Actually that's one of the things that I'm supposed to do well! Great. OK, the song is *(announces the next song)*.

Song: Here we go up to Bethlehem

Between verses the angel suddenly leaves announcing:

Angel:	I'm off to Bethlehem – *that's* where I'm supposed to be!
Minister:	Now that the angel's gone we'll be able to do our service … You'll be on soon children! *(to the nativity group)*. In fact *(glances at wristwatch)* – oh dear, maybe if we cut out the sermon; we're short of time now, with all these angel interruptions. *(Announces the next song.)*

Song: Mary had a baby

Angel:	*(standing next to Young person B now)* I'm ever so sorry, but I was off to Bethlehem and then I realised that I didn't really know the way; and I was listening to your song. It said: 'Mary had a baby and put him in the manger.'
Young person B:	So how can I help you?

Angel:	Well, I'm not sure … You all seem so kind, I was wondering if you could tell me more. You see, now I know that something is going on in Bethlehem with this baby Jesus, I keep wondering what I'm supposed to do there.
Young person B:	Well …

The angel suddenly knocks a Bible off a pew.

Angel:	Oh dear, oh dear. Now I've done it! … *(Picks it up)* What is this book anyway?
Young person B:	It's a Bible. You know, it might tell us what you need to know!
Angel:	Great, good! Well, what does it say?
Young person B:	Just a minute … Here it is … The reading for today … It's written by Luke … The story of the birth of Jesus. *(Reads Luke 2: 7–14)* … So what do you think?
Angel:	*(quietly)* Well, I love singing. Maybe if I turn up with a new song for the Chief Angel Gabriel it won't matter so much that I'm late. Could you teach me one?
Young person B:	Well, perhaps we can find one that we can all sing with you. Look, here's one about 'telling everyone' – we can sing it now, with everybody here, if you like?

Song: Go tell it on the mountain

Minister:	*(Glances at wristwatch)* Well, we're getting through the songs OK. *(To the congregation)* I hope you can all bear with us, I honestly don't think I've ever had so many interruptions. Still, we can get on with our nativity story now. Let's see, yes, the shepherds are out in the fields …
Shepherds:	*(together)* It's cold out tonight. Yes, and we need our supper soon. All the sheep are safely in and we –
Angel:	Hello, look it's the shepherds! I must be close now!
Shepherds:	*(together)* Hello, it's another one of those angels. What are you doing here? The others have all gone!

Angel:	Oh no, I can't bear it! First of all I oversleep and miss the meeting with Gabriel, then I go to the church and I find out about Mary and Joseph, Bethlehem, and the baby Jesus being born in a stable and his mum laying him in the manger. I even find out I'm supposed to be singing – and now you say all the angels have gone!
Shepherds	*(together):* We're off to see the baby Jesus in Bethlehem. We'll show you the way if you want.
Angel:	Gosh, I mean, thanks. I'd love to go.
	The shepherds move off down the aisle. The angel suddenly remembers the alarm clock and looks anxiously around for it. She/he goes up to lectern and, in the process, misses the shepherds leaving. The angel starts to cry. The minister comes forward.
Minister:	Haven't you found the way to the stable yet?
Angel:	No … I'll never find it. The angels have all gone and the shepherds will be there by now.
Minister:	Well, there are other people here who can help. Let's ask them. Shall we help the angel? Now, children, when you came in, did someone give you something, or did you make something before the service? Could you hold these up please, all of you?
	The children hold up their stars.
Minister:	Brilliant, thank you. Now it's the adults' turn. Can you please read out to us what it says on the top of your service sheet? … *(This is read out.)* Did you hear that, angel? … No? Adults, please speak up.
Angel:	If everyone said it together I'd hear the words.
Everyone:	Follow the star!
Angel:	*(moving to the pews)* But which one? The stars are lovely, but I need to find the one that leads me to Jesus.
	The lights go dim. The star, held up by the star-holder, is lit up behind the angel.
Angel:	Where is the star?
Everyone:	*(led by the minister and the cast)* It's behind you! It's behind you!

The angel spins around.

The lights go out completely. The people in the nativity scene, and all the angels, move into place or somewhere more central.

The lights come up on the nativity scene.

Song: In the deep midwinter *(or another suitable song) sung solo by the Angel*

Minister: Let us pray.

All: *Prayer (on back of the service sheet)*
Dear God,
thank you for this time together.
Thank you for the angel
who has helped us to think about Christmas.
Show us how to look for and follow the star
so that we can find you in our hearts and in our lives.
Amen

Minister: Angel, I'm glad you interrupted us – do come again sometime.

Angel: Thank you. Thank you everyone.

Song: The Virgin Mary had a baby boy

Karen Reeves

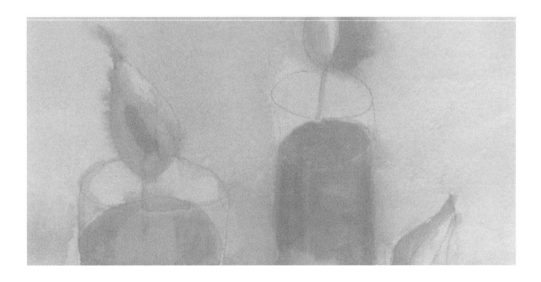

ONLY GOD WOULD CHRISTEN HIM JESUS

From da Noust: members and friends of the L'Arche Community Edinburgh

Characters:

Two women	*Anna*
Three wise men: Melchior, Caspar, Balthasar	*King Herod*
The innkeeper	*At least three shepherds*
The innkeeper's spouse	*Joseph*
The high priest	*Mary and their baby*
Simeon	

Music

Two original songs, O shoot of Jesse *and* Only God would christen Jesus, *are included here. Carols, known to the community, could also be included and/or substituted after each scene.*

Note: *When da Noust present this play some of the dialogue is signed.*

Scene one

Music to set the scene: first verse of O Shoot of Jesse, *instrumentally*

Two women (the wives of Melchior and Caspar) enter, shaking their heads and wringing their hands.

Woman 1:	Crazy.
Woman 2:	They're off their heads.
Woman 1:	The whole thing's mad. And I always said it was.
Woman 2:	A real wild goose chase. *(Pause)* And the cost of it.
Woman 1:	*(looks into the distance)* Ah well, they're away now – and a whole caravan of supplies with them.
Woman 2:	And all the servants.
Woman 1:	Off to Jerusalem – a month's trek each way. At least.
Woman 2:	In wintertime especially.
Woman 1:	You'd think one child would be enough for him, without chasing off after another one, even if it is some foreign royalty.
Woman 2:	Yes *(shakes her head)*.
Woman 1:	'A journey for truth,' he calls it. How he can say that and keep a straight face?

Sound of a baby crying

Ah, there's the babe waking.

The two women link arms in commiseration and go off together.

Song: O shoot of Jesse (or Immanuel)

Scene two: The inn

The innkeeper enters, apron on.

The three wise men enter with a retinue of servants (optional). One of the wise men carries a backpack with star maps sticking out of it.

Innkeeper:	Ah! *(rubbing his hands).* Good morning, gentlemen.
Melchior:	Good day. We are looking for a place to buy provisions.
Caspar:	And some shepherds pointed us to this village, for we are strangers here, and travellers.
Innkeeper:	Indeed. *(Aside)* Well, you're not the sort of travelling people I'm used to, not with those clothes and those fine animals. *(To the wise men)* You'll find nothing but the best in my stores. This place may be small, and some would say we're the least of the hill towns roundabouts – but we've plenty food, for man and beast. Come in out of the cold. You look like you've been travelling all night.
Balthasar:	Indeed we have. Our journey has led us to this unknown place – for we follow the light of a planet which rose like a star in the east.
Innkeeper:	A star indeed. *(Aside)* 'New age', I guess.
Caspar:	The star guides our journey.
Melchior:	*(eagerly)* Leading us to wisdom and truth.
Innkeeper:	Indeed …Well, this here is an inn, not some religious community. We've no time to go off looking for truth. But you'd best talk with folk wiser than me.
Balthasar:	Hush, Melchior.
Innkeeper:	Now, I'll be along for your food; and if you're needing a bed for the night, something might be arranged, though we're very busy round here, what with the census and all.
Balthasar:	No bed is needed *(the innkeeper looks disappointed)* but bring the food. The shepherds warned us that prices have risen since the crowds arrived.
Innkeeper:	Never trust a shepherd.
	The innkeeper's spouse enters from the other side of the acting space.
Spouse:	There's two more poor travellers just arrived at the door with nowhere to stay …
Innkeeper:	Tell them we've no room at the inn.

Spouse looks like he/she is about to protest, but bites lip, and exits the other way, thoughtfully. The innkeeper exits.

Melchior: Let's press on now, Balthasar, and not wait for the night. The star couldn't have stopped here. We seem to be headed towards Jerusalem. It's not really far – it can't be more than a few hours.

Caspar: And we know Jerusalem is the holy city – and the place of the king's court.

Melchior: And the temple … Where else would you look for a sign from God? Oh, come on. We can't stay in this hovel all day. *(Melchior leaves.)*

Balthasar, unsure, looks at Caspar who nods, and they exit together.

Spouse re-enters.

Spouse: Oh, I can't, I just can't send them away. What a journey they've had, in bitter bleak midwinter. I saw him with her on the donkey as they came over the brae – cuddling her, murmuring a song. She's at her time. There'll be a new child born tonight. The only question is where … I guess we'll have to make do with the stable. Good job it's not full up with the animals of those rich folk after all.

Song

Scene three: Jerusalem, the temple

Caspar, Melchior and Balthasar reverse into view as if pushed from offstage. An empty chair is front left.

Caspar: Well!

Melchior: Rough work *(dusting down his robes)*.

Caspar: Somehow I don't think we will be allowed into the inner court of the temple.

Melchior: The guards are strict – the second I let slip where we're from –

Caspar: 'No foreigners, no foreigners' *(quoting)*.

Melchior: And no women, no children, and no people with disabilities either … You wonder who that leaves in a place of worship.

Caspar:	And what a place it is – the size of the walls and columns *(gazing around)*. Sixteen years they've been building it and it's not even half-finished. The crowds of people too. It must be a special feast day.
Balthasar:	But where does that leave our search? I'm afraid we have blundered. There is no star here.

The high priest enters briskly; stops.

High priest:	Ah, gentlemen … *(He bows obsequiously. The wise men gravely return the bow.)* Gentlemen, I must apologise for your rough handling. I trust you are not too put out. It was reported to me that three strangers from foreign lands had made their way to our temple, speaking of the stars and the kingdoms of heaven.
Caspar:	We have journeyed far, through deserts and rocky places.
Melchior:	Skirting towns and travelling onwards.
Caspar:	Searching for a God among us – who we believe will be revealed to those of us who trek by the light of the stars.
Melchior:	And especially the sign that heralds a newborn king.
High priest:	A king indeed. Most interesting. Our own seers have recently predicted a new star in the sky too – but no king is born here in Jerusalem I can assure you. King Herod is well. And he does not lack a son and heir … *(Under his breath)* Though he used to have four sons, till he murdered three of them, and their mother.
Balthasar:	The heavenly body is only a sign. We have searched the scriptures of many peoples to try to understand what it means. We have listened to the voice of the prophet who said: 'Awake Jerusalem, shine out, for your light has come and the glory of God rises upon you, even though night still covers the earth.'
High priest:	Ah, so you know our own prophet Isaiah. He writes so beautifully of that dawning radiance which we ourselves are enclosing in this magnificent temple, finer than the one built by Solomon even. Each year sees new courtyards added around the holy of holies. Our children will live to see it finished. And each day worship is given to the one true God.

Balthasar:	Old men see visions, and young men dream dreams.
High priest:	And the Spirit of God is poured out on all. Why, just this year the priest, whose turn it was to enter the holy of holies, was struck dumb by a vision from God, such is the power of this place.
Caspar:	What did the vision show?
High priest:	That the priest, an old man well on in years, would have a first-born son, which, nine months later, he did. The priest has retired in shock of course, but I expect great things will come of the child.
Melchior:	Is he the Christ child, then? The anointed one.
High priest:	Oh no – his name is John. No one born in poverty, even priestly poverty, could be the one anointed King. That child will never over-throw Herod or his children.
Melchior:	So who is the Christ child?
High priest:	No one knows his name.
Caspar:	But we will not stop travelling till we find him.
High priest:	Yes … *(An idea strikes him).* I think that King Herod the Great may wish to meet you. We could compare the results of your star-gazing with that of our own seers. You must wait here in Jerusalem. He will see you within a week.
Caspar:	A week! But we must travel on tonight. We must follow the sign now.
High priest:	The star, yes … Well, opinion seems divided as to whether it stands exactly over Jerusalem or not, but it's as near as makes no difference. And you would *not* insult the hospitality of the king I hope?
Melchior:	*(reluctantly)* Indeed not. We are your guests.

The wise men look at each other. The high priest leaves. Balthasar sits down, and puts his head in his hands.

Scene four: The temple

Simeon enters.

Simeon:	(*urgently*) Strangers and friends, take care. I am Simeon – and I have heard that King Herod means to question you.
Caspar:	We journey in search of truth and fear no one.
Simeon:	Noble words, but I fear that no king of Judea has ever had much respect for truth. Beware Herod. Your journey is the talk of the city, and Herod will not rest while you carry on speaking of a newborn king. Why, his own son is fifteen years old!
Caspar:	But we have followed the star that rose in the east. We have read the scriptures: 'Arise, O Jerusalem, for kings will come to your dawning brightness.'
Simeon:	You look for light in the temple? Myself, I'm not so sure. I have spent my life near to the temple longing for the consolation of Israel, when God will visit his people.
Balthasar:	But the child who we are seeking, what is his name?
Simeon:	No one knows. But wait. Who's that?

Anna enters, skipping with joy.

Anna:	I knew it, I knew it! Praise God!
Simeon:	Anna! What's happening? Slow down!
Anna:	I spoke to one of the shepherds, calling down to him from the temple walls – you know, the shepherds who travel up and down the hill-country of Judea with their sheep?
Simeon:	And?
Anna:	And he told me what he's seen this very night: In Bethlehem, the old city of David – a baby, wrapped in swaddling clothes, and lying in a manger. And his parents – that very couple from Galilee that we met in here at the start of the festival three days ago.
Simeon:	Hmm … I remember them well: the mother young, very young, and full of courage, and the father a joiner by trade, short on words till you got to know him.

Anna: And so gentle with his wife. Mary she's called.

Simeon: Gentle as well with the story he told of their pregnancy and journey, and his own storm-tossed dreams about Mary. All that he went through, suspecting force and violence, and fearing consent.

Anna: *(firmly)* The child is a gift of God … Simeon, could this be the Christ?

Simeon: Should we go and see?

Anna: No. My call is to wait here.

Balthasar: We will go for you. We have gifts to give the Christ child – the spice of grief and three crowns of gold. All given to point the way.

Melchior: We thought our journey's end lay here in the temple of God – not in some shelter for poor people.

Balthasar: Yes, it's all so strange. *(Thinking)* Are we all called to look again at why we journey, the people we left behind, our homes?

Melchior: My wife …

Caspar: *(slowly)* My child …

Anna: Two women, two babies …

Simeon: Immanuel, God with us now.

Scene five: The temple

Herod steals in from a dark corner.

King Herod: God indeed be with us. Gentlemen, magi, I am pleased to meet you.

The wise men step back. Anna and Simeon disappear.

Balthasar: King Herod, I presume.

   Herod regards him frostily.

Balthasar: King Herod, the Great.

King Herod: Indeed! *(Beams)* Magi, you will be made welcome in my palace while we study together the charts you have made of the stars and planets. We can talk of kingdoms and truth. I need your charts to compare with mine. The fools I pay to look at the skies could not even tell me when that bright planet first appeared – even though it is right over our heads! 'Too close to the sun,' they moan, 'we can't see it any more.'

Balthasar: We are happy to compare records – but then we must journey on, for we have not found what we are looking for in this place.

King Herod: Well, we're all keeping a look out for a newborn king. *(Slyly)* Promise me you will send me word if you find him, and I guarantee you'll be away from here within a week, with all your charts too.

Balthasar: We will share the news with everyone who wishes to pay homage.

King Herod: Done! Hand me your charts!

Caspar takes out the star charts and hands them over reluctantly.

King Herod: Come with me to my palace.

They exit together. The melody of the song 'Over my head'(Love & Anger, Wild Goose Publications) or a Gloria starts up, and continues until the beginning of the next scene.

Scene six: Outside the stable

A group of shepherds assemble (on a lower level of the acting space, if possible).

Shepherd 1: I could nae believe it. There we were, out in the open, another cold night, and suddenly there was music and light all around.

Shepherd 2: And a whole gaggle of folk up there singing.

Straight away, illuminated on a higher level (if possible), a group of angels appears. The actors playing the angels are dressed in bright clothes.

The angels sing 'Over my head' or a well-known Gloria.

A dance by some of the angels (optional)

Angels continue to hum quietly, as the shepherds talk and move around the acting space, ending up at the stable finally.

Shepherd 1: And there we all were in a dwam*. Could nae believe it.

Shepherd 2:   Walking down the brae into Bethlehem, the city of David.

Shepherd 1:   Normally we'd never go near it. *(Quoting)* 'Shepherds out! Not welcome here.'

Shepherd 2:   Walking into the village, to look for a sign.

Shepherd 1:   A baby, wrapped in the clothes of a newborn and lying in a manger.

Shepherd 2:   We didnae ken his name even.

Shepherd 1:   But when we get there … *(They arrive at stable.)*

Shepherd 2:   Hearts burstin' with joy!

Shepherd 1:   We the shepherds, the nobodies, the fourth world of the people, we kent him – Jesse's stock, a son of David, a royal child.

Shepherd 2:   But with parents like ourselves.

Shepherd 1:   Same standing.

Shepherd 2:   Fourth world of the people – refugees even.

Shepherd 1:   A homeless couple with their child.

Shepherd 2:   With no room at the inn to spare.

Shepherd 1:   Their child born of David's line.

Shepherd 2:   Though few will know his worth.

Shepherd 1:   They've welcomed weakness …

Shepherd 2:   God's sign of covenant love.

Song

Scene seven: The stable

Enter shepherds carrying candles or lanterns.

Shepherd 1:   And that was one week ago. We've been back every day of course. They're doing well for a first child, and he doesn't greet* *too* much.

Shepherd 2:	We're all invited back for today, the eighth – his naming day. The kids are excited. They've not let on about the name at all, so we're all guessing … Samuel, Benjamin, Joseph, of course? There's plenty dads who would name him after themselves.
Shepherd 1:	The rabbi's been in to mark him with the sign of Abraham. You should have heard the greetin' then!
	Actors gather, with shepherds to one side and Joseph and Mary next to the crib, so that both face the next guests to enter. Singers are gathered at the back.
Mary:	Is everything ready, Joseph?
	Joseph takes a candle or lantern from one of the shepherds and gives it to Mary to hold. He picks up the baby.
Mary:	Thank you everyone for coming to share his name day. You are all part of his family now.
	Silence
Joseph:	I name this child, Jesus.
	A tinkle of bells from offstage
Shepherd 1:	Only Joseph would name him 'Jesus'.
Shepherd 2:	With a name that means 'God saves' – saviour of all pilgrim people … *(He stares into the distance.)* But what's this?
Shepherd 1:	Caravans of wealth appearing – animals laden with riches.
Shepherd 2:	They're no shepherds from some lowland shieling … The high road only for them.
Shepherd 1:	I think it's those magi we sent on some days past, gazing up at the stars.

Song

Balthasar:	We have come to greet the newborn king.
Youngest shepherd:	Why are they late then?

Shepherd 1:	Hush, the kings must have come a long way.
Shepherd 2:	*(ironically)* As rich folk often do.
Balthasar:	Yes, to give up our plans and privilege – and dream of new journeys.
Melchior:	The gifts we thought of giving are only a small part of our possessions.
Caspar:	But the gifts we need to receive now are the ones that come from God: forgiveness from my wife and child.
Melchior:	Community restored.
Balthasar:	And the courage to turn for home by unknown ways, avoiding Herod.
Melchior:	Who plans evil for this child.
Caspar:	Beware, Joseph. We sense violence in the air. Herod's soldiers will bring heartache.
Balthasar:	Please take our gifts for your journey: the spice of grief, three crowns of gold, and perfume to scent an entire home with a blessing.

Song

Incense is lit from offstage.

During the song, the magi present their gifts to Jesus. The candle/lantern that Mary is holding is set beside the crib. After Mary and Joseph unwrap the gifts, the two women from scene one, the wives of Melchior and Caspar (holding a baby), step out of the shadows and embrace their husbands in turn. Simeon and Anna then appear on one side of the acting space, while King Herod, alone, appears on the opposite side, clutching and studying his star charts. The innkeeper and spouse come in at the back.

Mary:	Joseph, we must at least go back to the temple to see Simeon and Anna.
Balthasar:	But keep away from Herod. *(All look over to Herod, then back towards Simeon and Anna.)*

Joseph nods. He and Mary, holding baby Jesus, get up and leave.

Shepherd 1:	Your home – it's in the arms of your parents.

Shepherd 2:   They'll hold you close – close enough to hear your heartbeat.

Shepherd 1:   *(calls after them)* Mary! Joseph!

Shepherd 2:   Only God would christen him Jesus.

Song: *Either* Only God would christen Jesus *or* The shepherds' farewell *(Berlioz), followed by* Over my head, *with all the actors gathered together at the front of the stage.*

da Noust

(*da* Noust are members and friends of L'Arche, Edinburgh)

* dwam – daze
* greet – cry

SONGS

O shoot of Jesse
(Tune: Song 24, Orlando Gibbons (or another with a metre 10.10.10.10.10.10))

O shoot of Jesse in this time did spring,
O weakness welcomed by our servant king,
O wisdom of our God, ordaining all;
Come now to teach us in the way of truth.
You gave the law on Sinai's desert height:
Come here and save us with your outstretched hand.

O sapling thrusting from the severed root,
On him the breath of God, the Spirit, rests;
His verdict fair, he judges for the poor,
His word a rod that strikes the proud of heart.
Here waters swell the sea, the lands rejoice;
And Jesse's stem will be for God a voice.

O Key of David, open now the gate;
You come to free all those whose heart is bound,
To liberate from jails of sin and hate;
O Morning Star, who burns with healing light,
Transfigure all who live in fear of death;
Emmanuel, Amen, Alleluia.

Emmanuel, our King and cornerstone,
A first-born child of parents far from home,
Who wait for you in word and dream-born trust,
Their Advent journey filled with hope and fear;
They long for you, the promise of their love:
Delay no more, reveal God's covenant.

Only God would christen Jesus
(Tune: Quem pastores)
(best sung with two sets of alternating voices)

Only God would christen Jesus
With a name that faith reveals as
    Saviour of all pilgrim people –
    Those who trek by silver light.

Caravans of wealth appearing;
Shepherds come from lowland shielings;
    No one knew his name was Jesus –
    God with us in human need.

Heartbeat close, his parents cradle
Jesus, born within a stable;
    See the cult of power disabled –
    God is born for human kind.

Stars appear and promise daybreak,
Violent soldiers herald heartache;
    Cries of anguish pierce the darkness;
    Where is God in human need?

Word made flesh, our gifts revealing,
Mary, Joseph, persevering,
    All who find God's gift amazing
    Turn for home by unknown ways.

SAINT STEPHEN'S DAY

Lectionary readings

Acts 6:8–10; 7:54–59; Psalm 31; Matthew 10:17–22

ON ST STEPHEN'S DAY

These days our stones are cynicism and indifference,
ignorance and faint praise.
Also bigotry and fanaticism,
narrow minds and closed hearts.

Give us grace to build, not destroy.
Open heaven and bring your kingdom now.

Nick Burden

RESPONSES

Look!
Sunshine, white waves,
trees in winter,
birds in the garden,
SEE GOD'S GLORY

Look!
A child being born,
adults at play,
a hand reaching to heaven,
SEE GOD'S GLORY

Look!
Courage in darkness,
a hug on a journey,
a smile of forgiveness,
SEE GOD'S GLORY

Living in us
GOD
Listening to us
GOD
Believing in us
GOD
Speaking through us
GOD

Whatever we do
WE ARE ALWAYS IN YOUR CARE

Wherever we go
WE ARE ALWAYS IN YOUR CARE

Every moment of our days
WE ARE ALWAYS IN YOUR CARE

In our living and our dying
WE ARE ALWAYS IN YOUR CARE.

Ruth Burgess

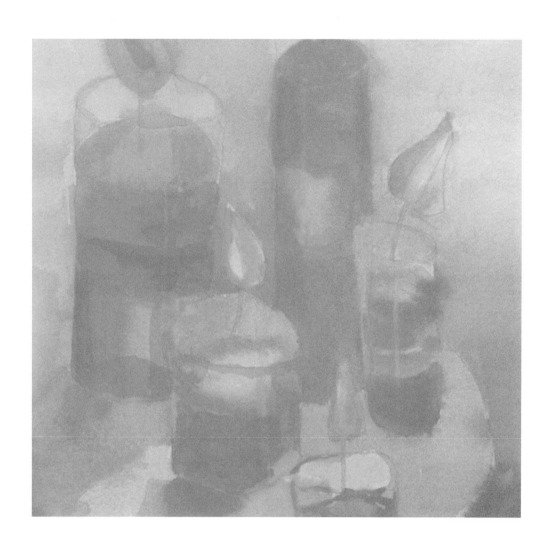

HOLY FAMILY

Lectionary readings

Year A
Ecclesiastes 3:2–6,12–14; Psalm 128; Colossians 3:12–21; Matthew 2:13–23

Year B
Genesis 15:1–6; 21:1–3; Psalm 105; Hebrews 11:18; Luke 2:22–40

Year C
1 Samuel 1:20–22,24–28; Psalm 84; 1 John 3:1–2,21–24; Luke2:41–52

A SERIES OF RESPONSES

Single people
Divorced people
Married people
GOD IS AT HOME IN YOU

Children
Parents
Elders
GOD IS AT HOME IN YOU

Widows
Widowers
Orphans
GOD IS AT HOME IN YOU

> Among family
> and friends
> WE HAVE LOOKED FOR YOU

> Among travellers
> and strangers
> WE HAVE LOOKED FOR YOU

> Among teachers
> and preachers
> WE HAVE LOOKED FOR YOU

> You worry us
> and question us
> AND WE DO NOT UNDERSTAND YOU

Through darkness
Through danger
WE WILL COME SAFE HOME

Through night stars
and daylight
WE WILL COME SAFE HOME

With saints
and angels
WE WILL COME SAFE HOME

To God
To heaven
WE WILL COME SAFE HOME

   With prayer
   With ceremony
   LET US GO IN PEACE

   With wisdom
   With wonder
   LET US GO IN PEACE

   With love
   With justice
   LET US GO IN PEACE

Deep wisdom
GROW IN US

Integrity
GROW IN US

Holiness
GROW IN US

GROW IN US
AND BRING FORTH FRUIT

Ruth Burgess

GOD, IN YOUR MERCY

God, Saviour of the world, who was born as a human child in Bethlehem –
there is no room for you at the inn.
We pray for all who are rejected, all for whom there is no home, no welcome.
We pray for those who are outcasts in today's world,
through poverty, hunger and oppression.
God, in your mercy,
HEAR OUR PRAYER.

God, Lord of the world, who fled to Egypt as a refugee,
we pray for all refugees, all who are fleeing their homeland in fear,
who have left behind people they love and everything that is familiar to them.
Help us to do our part in welcoming and supporting them.
God, in your mercy,
HEAR OUR PRAYER.

God, Prince of peace,
we pray for peace in our world.
We pray especially at this time for … *(countries, people)*
And we pray for the leaders of the nations,
for those who are faced with the huge problem of bringing an end
to violence and warfare.
God, in your mercy,
HEAR OUR PRAYER.

God, Father of us all, we pray for this church and this neighbourhood.
Help us to remember that we are all members of your family.
Help us to welcome all who come among us,
knowing that in showing love and respect to any member of your family
we are showing it to you.
God, in your mercy,
HEAR OUR PRAYER.

We pray for people who are sick in body or in mind,
and especially for those known to us personally.
In their need may they know your healing touch.
God, in your mercy,
HEAR OUR PRAYER.

God of salvation, peace and justice,
you come to us now as you have come to your people in every age.
We thank you for all who have reflected the life of Christ.
Help us to follow their example, and bring us, with them, to eternal life.
Amen

Irene Barratt

HEAR OUR PRAYER

God of love and wonder,
we, your children,
bring you our hopes and prayers:

We pray for those who live in countries and cultures that are unfamiliar,
for refugees, for those who seek asylum.
We pray for family members who live apart from one another.
We pray for those who come to Britain seeking shelter and hope.
God, in your mercy,
HEAR OUR PRAYER.

We pray for families.
We remember that Jesus did not always agree with his parents
and that his parents worried about him.
We pray for love and justice in family relationships …
for homes that are safe spaces for questions and laughter and tears.
God, in your mercy,
HEAR OUR PRAYER.

We pray for our local communities and churches.
We rejoice in Christmas trees on council roundabouts
and candles in dark places.
God, in your mercy,
HEAR OUR PRAYER.

We pray for those who are sick, or in need, or in any kind of trouble.
We remember friends and family members who have died …
Tell them how much we love them and miss them …
God, in your mercy,
HEAR OUR PRAYER.

We pray for ourselves … for our needs, our hopes, our dreams …
God, in your mercy,
HEAR OUR PRAYER.

God you love us.
We are your family.
Help us to love you,
and to live in wonder and justice
all our days. AMEN

Ruth Burgess

HIS PULSING FIST

His pulsing fist
kicks against my skin.
When all this is over
and I am rid of the shame,
we will return to Judea
where he will grow
strong and good and true.
Already I imagine myself
as an old woman
with him looking after me.

Rosie Miles

HOLY INNOCENTS

Lectionary readings

1 John 1:5–2:2; Psalm 124; Matthew 2:13–18

TO LIVE IN LIGHT
Opening responses

We are called
TO LIVE IN LIGHT

We are called
TO LIVE IN JUSTICE

We are called
TO WALK WITH GOD

Ruth Burgess

YOU SHARE OUR ANGER

When children are abused
YOU SHARE OUR ANGER

When children are in pain
YOU SHARE OUR DISTRESS

When children are murdered
YOU SHARE OUR HORROR

When children die
YOU SHARE OUR DESPAIR

God, who welcomes and cherishes children,
we bring you our prayers:

We pray for children living and dying in places of fear and violence,
for children dying of hunger and disease.
God, in your mercy,
HEAR OUR PRAYER.

We pray for children who have been abducted from their homes,
for children who are pawns in political games.
God, in your mercy,
HEAR OUR PRAYER.

We pray for children who are tortured and abused,
for children whose lives are short and full of pain.
God, in your mercy,
HEAR OUR PRAYER.

We pray for parents who have to watch their children die,
for parents who are unable to keep their children safe.
God, in your mercy,
HEAR OUR PRAYER.

We pray for children and parents and guardians in our midst,
for all who love them and support them.
God, in your mercy,
HEAR OUR PRAYER.

Ruth Burgess

GOD OF EARTH AND HEAVEN
Closing prayer

God of earth and heaven,
in times of pain
and in times of plenty,
we seek your blessing.
Lay your hands on us in love
and give good gifts to your children.
In Jesus' name and in the love of the Holy Spirit we pray. Amen

Ruth Burgess

YOUR CHILD'S COMING WAS MY CHILD'S GOING

Words and tune: Ian M Fraser. Arranged by Nicholas Williams.

Your child's coming was my child's going,
Mary, Mary;
Swift appeared the soldier band,
Children's blood spilled on the sand,
Grief and rage convulsed the land –
Mary, Mary,
Was your child born
That Rachel weep forlorn?

Your child's living was my child's dying,
Mary, Mary;
Days hang loose like cloth unshrunk,
Nights are haunted, anguish-sunk,
Breasts are pained, the milk not drunk –
Mary, Mary,
Was your child worth
Mine laid in friendless earth?

Your child's saving was mine's destroying,
Mary, Mary;
Cherished limbs have lost their power,
Cherished hopes have now turned sour,
Cherished seed will not find flower –
Mary, Mary,
If Jesus saves,
What mean to you these graves?

Ian M Fraser

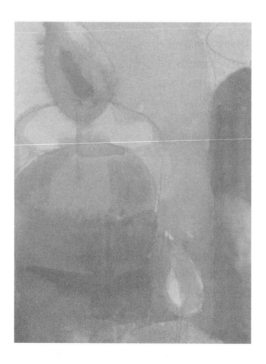

HEROD

O I promised them! I spoke them sweet.
I spilled soft words upon their ears
saying nothing of my private fears.
I said, 'You must journey on and greet
this newborn king, and then must journey back again
and bring me news, that I may also go and worship him.'

Who gave the game away? How did they know?
How could they guess? From what source did they learn?
Whatever happened, they did not return;
there was no information, nothing to show.
And no address. A pity – the damage could have been less.
As it was, I'm afraid, we made a bloody mess.

I sent my soldiers out with orders to, well, kill
all male children up to two years old.
I know such action makes me seem quite cold.
But I'm a king, I've a duty to fulfil;
you have to see, it's a matter of national security.
And I can't allow a child to grow to rival me.

It's only little people with their little lives
that can afford to take a moral stand.
I have to think what's best for all this land.
So, yes, there were some unimportant Hebrew wives
that wept and wailed for their little Hebrew males.
But what matters is *my* place is unassailed.

Penny Hewlett

THE INNKEEPER'S WIFE

We had just lit the lamps when they knocked. Reuben answered the door, as he always did after dark. He was a very careful man. We had only been married for a couple of years and were still struggling to build up the business. But we were becoming known and had a few regulars who stayed whenever they were in town. Of course, with the census that week, there were some strange people about and everywhere was full. I wasn't surprised to hear Reuben tell the caller that we had no room left and that he would have to look elsewhere. It served him right, I thought. He shouldn't have left it so late. Then I heard him speak; a rough, country voice made harsh by weariness and worry:

'Surely you could find us a corner where my wife could rest for a while,' he pleaded.

Now Reuben was much too soft-hearted, especially when there was a pretty girl involved. I knew he'd take pity on them if I didn't intervene. It wasn't that I was hard-hearted, but Rachel was only six months old and I was exhausted. I couldn't cope with any more visitors.

'Look for yourself,' I said, flinging the door wide. 'They're even sleeping under the tables.'

A wave of laughter and obscenities almost drowned my words as a group of drunken soldiers rolled out of the door, spooking the stranger's donkey and almost unseating his young wife. It was then that I noticed her condition. She should never have had to leave home when she was so near her time. I could understand her husband's anxiety: she was grey with fatigue and almost falling from the saddle. But there was nowhere we could put them, and I didn't want the responsibility if it was a difficult birth.

Then I thought of Daniel and Miriam. Their place was in the next street; their stable backed onto ours. They might be able to fit them in. Reuben gave me a strange look when I suggested it, then shrugged and gave the man directions. I assumed that that was the last we would hear of them. Would that it had been!

I didn't sleep well that night. I couldn't get the girl's face out of my mind. What if Daniel and Miriam had turned them away as well? It was far too cold for anyone to sleep out in the fields, especially a woman in her condition. I began to wish I hadn't been so hasty.

I hurried round to Miriam's as soon as I could get away the next morning. I wasn't surprised to learn that the baby, a boy, had been born during the night. Miriam was looking as pleased as if she were the mother. She took me through to the stable to see him. It didn't seem right, giving birth in a stable among all the animals, but the family seemed quite comfortable and, as Miriam said, there really was no place else. Mind you, I was horrified when I saw that the girl had put the baby into the manger, just wrapped in a cloak and with the animals pulling wisps of hay out from around him; although he certainly appeared quite contented. I wasn't so sure about the girl though. I know we all think our babies are special, but she kept telling everyone that he was the Son of God. It was so embarrassing.

Then the strangest folk started turning up and demanding to see the baby. First there was a band of rough-looking fellows from up in the hills, claiming to be shepherds. They knocked at our door first.

'We've come to see the Christ child,' said one old chap, leaning heavily on a thumb stick.

Reuben threatened to set the dogs on them if they didn't clear off. But they were persistent.

'We followed the star as the angel told us to.'

Reuben seemed to think that they had had too much wine on the way to town, but I did begin to wonder, especially when the next lot arrived. They were really peculiar, three foreigners, quite well-off by the look of them, with six or seven servants. You could tell by their clothes that they had travelled some distance. Miriam said she could hardly understand a word they said, their accents were so thick. She said they had brought all sorts of expensive presents with them.

They stayed three nights and I couldn't believe Miriam when she told me how much they had spent. She and Daniel probably made more in those three days than they had in the previous three months.

Then, suddenly, the man disappeared with his wife and baby in the middle of the night. They left money to pay for their lodging but, as Miriam said, that wasn't the point. It wasn't polite just to go like that, without saying goodbye or thank you.

Of course, we soon found out why.

The town had emptied quickly once the census was over. Reuben had gone off with the other men to replenish our provisions, and I was alone in the house with Rachel when it happened.

It was early in the morning and Rachel was still asleep in her cradle. I had just lit the fire and was about to get dressed. The sticks were starting to crackle and I remember hearing a donkey braying. Suddenly, as I was pulling my gown over my head, the door slammed open so violently that plaster crashed to the floor. Two soldiers with drawn swords burst in while a third stood in the doorway, watching the street. Before I could shout out I was flung against the wall with a hairy forearm across my throat and the point of a sword pricking my belly through the cloth of my gown. The smell of the soldier's breath made me want to retch. I clawed at his face and tried to scream. He struck me across the temple with the hilt of his sword.

When I recovered consciousness my first reaction was relief that I had not been raped. Then I heard the screaming and wailing coming from outside. I struggled to my feet and staggered to Rachel's cradle. I think I knew before I reached it what I would find. My screams joined those of all the other mothers whose children had been murdered that morning.

'I don't understand,' Reuben kept saying when he returned home. 'Why kill the children? Why kill the children?!'

Once you thought about it, it was obvious. One of the soldiers had been shouting something about there not being any King of the Jews now. Maybe all those strange visitors had been right, and that girl's baby was the Son of God. But it seemed incredible. We all knew that the Messiah would come one day, but surely he wouldn't be born in a stable. But Herod must have believed it, or why send soldiers to kill all the children? Someone else must have believed it as well and warned his parents. But no one warned us. Rachel had had no chance to escape.

'But she was a *girl*,' Reuben kept saying.

There are some who will tell you that only baby boys were killed, or that the soldiers were acting under orders and had no choice. They weren't there. It was planned down to the last detail. The soldiers were in place before dawn. They broke into every house at the same time. They killed every baby and toddler they saw, and every adult who tried to stop them, and then left before people realised what had happened.

Most people never got over it. There was such sadness and anger in the town that I grew to dread people coming to the inn. All they could talk about was the massacre of the children. Some had lost more than one child and were inconsolable. Some parents, whose children had been old enough to escape, were made to feel guilty.

Of course we all knew who had given them shelter; and what made it even more unfair was that Daniel and Miriam had no children. They had made a handsome profit and we had paid the price. At first it was only abuse that was thrown at them, but soon it was stones and worse. Their windows were broken and their animals driven off. Obscenities were daubed on their walls and door in blood. Finally their inn was set on fire. They escaped with what they could carry and fled the town. I don't know where they went. I didn't want to know. I was just so relieved that it hadn't been us who had given that woman shelter. I don't think I could have lived with the guilt.

Reuben never recovered from losing Rachel. He became irritable and depressed. He would sit all day drinking and staring into the fire, or would disappear for hours at a time. One afternoon, as winter was drawing near again, he went out and didn't return. A neighbour found him the next morning and brought him home, soaking wet and chilled to the bone. By the following day he had a raging fever, and before the end of the week he was dead.

Eventually I remarried and made a new life for myself in Jerusalem. Jacob is a good man and has cared for me well. I've borne his children, whom I love dearly, and I've tried to put the past behind me. But I have never forgotten Rachel and Reuben.

Marjorie Tolchard

HERODANDTHECHILDREN

Words: Leith Fisher. Music: John L Bell

Hear now, the cry   is sad and wild,
This is the world   Christ came to save,

Ra - chel la - ments   for her lost child,
The world he took   down to the grave.

As blight - ed hopes and   sa - vage pain
He bears our pain, and   through his load,

Dark - en the world of   now and then.
Brings to our wounds the   love of God.

Hear now, the cry is sad and wild,
Rachel laments for her lost child,
as blighted hopes and savage pain
darken the world of now and then.

This is the world Christ came to save,
the world he took down to the grave.
He bears our pain and, through his load,
brings to our wounds the love of God.

Leith Fisher

PUTTING HEROD BACK INTO CHRISTMAS

We talk about putting Christ back into Christmas. We also need to put Herod back into Christmas. Far from spoiling the image, the Christmas story actually makes much more sense if we include the unpleasant aspects.

Perhaps it's because we don't want to upset the children, because we want to shield them. But lots of bad things happen and children know about them. To include in the Christmas story the slaughter of the innocents only serves to show that Jesus was born into the real world. Horrible though it was, it's no worse than many things that happen today. When we question God's whereabouts and intentions in the catastrophes of life there are no simple answers.

The Christmas story is fantastic but it's not fantasy. It's fantastic because of the good news that God became human. We turn it into fantasy if we make it all cosy and nice and avoid the uncomfortable bits. Cosy and nice is fine for a short while; it refreshes and relaxes us. But the good news is God in the midst of the light and the darkness, giving us strength and hope for the long haul of life.

Liz Gibson

(with thanks to Joy Carroll Wallis of the Sojourners Community, for the phrase 'putting Herod back into Christmas')

WEEP WITH US

On this Day of Holy Innocents we pray:

For those killed in times of war,
for those killed in accidents,
for those killed deliberately,
God, in your mercy,
HEAR OUR PRAYER

For parents whose children are dying,
for parents whose children have died,
for parents whose children are missing,
God, in your mercy,
HEAR OUR PRAYER

For those who give orders to kill,
for those who are trained to kill,
for those who have taken life,
God, in your mercy,
HEAR OUR PRAYER

For those who cannot let go of anger or guilt,
For those who weep today,
For those who will die today,
God, in your mercy,
HEAR OUR PRAYER

God of life and death and resurrection,
walk with us,
weep with us,
love us,
wipe away our tears.

Through light and through darkness,
bring all your children safely home. Amen

Ruth Burgess

WINTER AND NEW YEAR

SOMETHING WISE, SOMETHING JOYFUL

Walk wisely in this world.
Listen before you speak.
look deeply before you leap.
Share love with those who walk beside you.

And, on long winter nights
when the moon is hiding
and frost crusts the soil,
do not be afraid to try out something different,
something wild,
something joyful,
just for the hell of it
and hope that it leads you to heaven.

Ruth Burgess

INSTRUMENT OF PEACE

After St Francis

To the ice of hate
may I be an axe of love

to frostbitten injury
the salve of pardon

to cold waters of doubt
a bridge of faith

to the dark soil of despair
a seed of hope

to the snowstorm of sadness
a shelter of joy

to long nights of darkness
a lantern of light.

Mary Palmer

FROM THE DAMP

From the damp that lingers
and fingers our flesh,
God, in your warmth, deliver us.

From the mist that chides
and hides your joy,
God, in your light, illumine us.

From winter's sleep that chills
and stills our strength,
God, in your morning, waken us.

Ruth Burgess

YEAR'S END

A small iron gate set in an old stone wall. I open it and walk into a wonderful meadow. During the early autumn months the trees are aflame with colour and the wind rustles through the leaves. Gnarled old oaks, what a story they could tell! By the end of October there are deep carpets of leaves lying in large circles around the trunks of the trees. As you push your feet through them they make a delicious crunching sound. One windy day I looked up and saw hundreds of golden leaves scudding through the air, like birds migrating before the winter comes.

Now, the trees are bare – beautiful flowing lines and shapes, so proud and so ancient. I hear a scuffing sound nearby and a large brown hare leaps majestically into the air. I watch him bounding over the wet tufts of grass, until he disappears suddenly into a dark patch of undergrowth.

Soon, a soft white blanket of winter mist will drift across this landscape, as November becomes December, and the air will feel fridge-cold and crisp against one's cheeks. The bare oak trees will be enveloped in the mist as a pale watery sun sinks lower towards the horizon and eventually disappears behind a thick grey blanket of cloud. Winter will have crept in quietly, settled herself, and stretched out frosty arms to greet the new year.

Pat Stubbs

WATCHNIGHT SERVICE PRAYER FROM IONA

God with us –
as the wind comes rushing through the darkness
across miles of wild ocean
and batters this building,
as the gales howl through the gaps
and hurl sleet against the windows,
we know that we are held safe,
out of this raging and wrathful world
in a sheltering place,
as though in the hollow of your hand:
strong and caring God.

God with us –
we know, too, that you are present
in the power of creation:
the energy of wind and water,
the majesty of Ben More crowned with snow,
the mystery of the night sky,
the intricate beauty of a shell.
On a day like this
we feel the beat of your heart;
on a night like this
we are so close, we hear you breathing,
and we are inspired, caught up in your life:
strong creative Spirit.

God with us –
on a day like this,
on a night like this;
in a place like this,
in a world like this –
a world of suffering and hope,
of tears and laughter –
at the turning of the year
we turn to you.

Jan Sutch Pickard

WE WOULD LET GO OF THE PAST

Eternal God,
Creator, Son and Spirit,
at the start of this new year,
with your help,
we would let go of the past.
We would lay down our failures, guilt and shame,
and lift up our eyes,
and look to the future.

Let the grace of your presence
strengthen our resolve,
enlighten our minds,
clarify our wills,
and inflame our hearts
with love for you
and for all people.

So may we live dedicated lives
in peace, and with courage, faith and cheerfulness,
until the year's end.
Through the grace of our Lord Jesus Christ. Amen

John Harvey

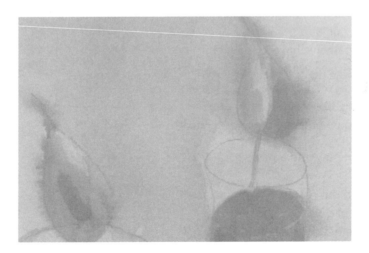

ALWAYS EMMANUEL

God, above time, above space,
yet with us and in us in Christ,
we who are creatures of time and space
come to you tonight
with thankfulness.

We give you thanks
for the year that is passing.
We thank you
for the many ways in which you have touched us,
in moments of great happiness
or in deep distress.
You have been present in Christ,
the Alpha and the Omega,
the beginning and the end.

We thank you
for the people who matter to us,
near and far,
who have given themselves to us
and through whom you have
been present to us
in their love.

We thank you for your church,
the community of faith
in whose company we have journeyed,
whose friendship we value,
whose challenge we welcome,
and whose wide boundaries
are not defined by time, by space or by death.

As we move on now into a new year,
give us grace
to leave behind our regrets and our failures
and any sense of guilt,
to let go of the past with gratitude,

and to leave in your hands the future in faith –
to live each moment
in joyful discipleship,
in the company of him
who is always Emmanuel,
God with us.
Amen

John Harvey

STEP SOFTLY

Step softly into your weeping world,
incarnate God;
embrace it in your love.
Bring light into broken lives,
warmth into frozen hearts,
hope to those at war.
May your peace pervade every place.

Help us to approach this new year
filled with the joy of your companionship,
as we step out in faith with you,
ready to face the future,
whatever it may hold.

Carol Dixon

LET US GIVE THANKS

Let us give thanks
at the start of this new year
for the many ways
in which our lives are supported
day by day.

For familiar shops and faces on the street,
for warm homes and full cupboards,
for friends and entertainment,
for new challenges and past achievements,
for good government and the absence of famine, plague or war,

We thank you Lord
AND PRAISE YOUR HOLY NAME.

Let us give thanks especially for those we love,
whose loyalty we depend upon,
whose faults and frailties we forgive,
whose acceptance of our faults and frailties we wonder at,
whose daily presence we so easily take for granted.
For dearest and nearest,
wherever they are,
whoever they are,
however they are,
we thank you Lord
AND PRAISE YOUR HOLY NAME. AMEN

John Harvey

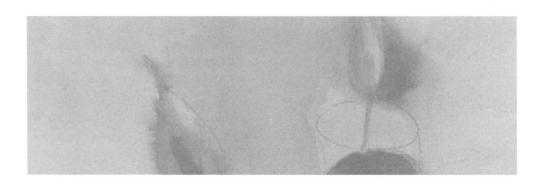

A BLESSING AS YOU JOURNEY INTO THE NEW YEAR

May your eyes be opened to the wonder of the daily miracles around you
and your sense of mystery be deepened.

May you be aware of the light that shines in the darkness,
and that the darkness can never put out.

May you be blessed with companions on the journey,
friends who will listen to you and encourage you with their presence.

May you learn to live with what is unsolved in your heart,
daring to face the questions and holding them
until, one day, they find their answers.

May you find the still, quiet place inside yourself
where you can know and experience the peace that passes understanding.

May love flow in you and through you to those who need your care.

May you continue to dream dreams and to reach out into the future
with a deeper understanding of God's way for you. Amen

Lynda Wright

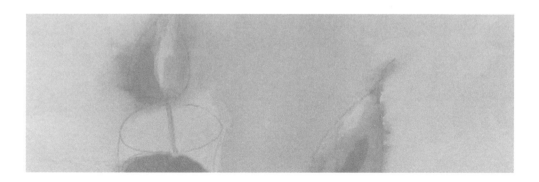

NEW YEAR BLESSING

We stand to face the future:

God behind us in the past;
Christ before us, the way ahead;
Christ beside us in this moment;
Christ beneath us in our weakness;
Christ above us to shield us –
beneath the shadow of his wings we are safe;
Christ between us to bind us in the unity of his love;
Christ in us, equipping us with his all-sufficient grace.

Thus armed, guided and protected we face the new year.

Now we arise and go forth on the journey before us,
knowing that, where Christ leads, life is a journey home.
Therefore we travel in faith, in hope, and in love,
in the name of the Father and of the Son and of the Holy Spirit.

May the blessing of God,
Father, Son and Holy Spirit,
be upon us
and upon all this year
and to all eternity. Amen

Ian Cowie

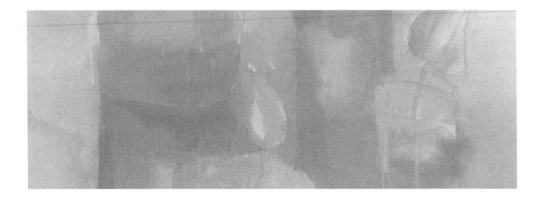

CHRIST, THE MORNING STAR

Through Christ, the firstborn of all creation,
WE PRAY FOR RESPECT FOR THE EARTH.

Through Christ, Prince of peace,
WE PRAY FOR PEACE FOR EARTH'S PEOPLES.

Through Christ, King of love,
WE PRAY FOR LOVE IN OUR LIVES.

Through Christ, Lord of the dance,
WE PRAY FOR DELIGHT IN THE GOOD.

Through Christ, divine healer,
WE PRAY FOR FORGIVENESS FOR PAST WRONGS.

Through Christ, Morning Star of a new year,
WE PRAY FOR THE GRACE TO MAKE A NEW START
FOR OURSELVES AND FOR OUR WORLD.

And may God bless us and keep us, today and each day.
And until we meet again, may God hold us in the palm of his hand.
AMEN

Wellspring

BENEDICTION

The blessing of the One who was, who is, and who is to come
be upon you all,
redeeming your past,
filling your present,
lighting up your future.
In the name of the Father, the Son and the Holy Spirit.
Amen

Ian Cowie

EPIPHANY

Lectionary readings

Isaiah 60:1–6; Psalm 72; Ephesians 3:2–3,5–6; Matthew 2:1–12

GLADLY WE COME TOGETHER

Gladly, O God, we come together,
here in this place,
to seek your deeper presence in the silence.

Silence

We bring before you
our wounds and our weariness
from the journey.

TOGETHER WE LOOK
WITH HOPEFUL EXPECTATION
TO FIND THE STAR
WHICH SIGNALS YOUR ARRIVAL.

Thankfully, we come forward
to kneel and to receive
the glory of your presence.

WITH OUR LITTLE GIFTS
WE ARE HUMBLED BEFORE YOU.

And we find among the straw,
in the misty breath of the animals,

THAT YOU HAVE COME MORE HUMANLY
THAN WE COULD IMAGINE.

Yvonne Morland

RESPONSES FOR EPIPHANY

Wise God
You are older than the ages
And you dance in the starlight
AND YOU LOVE US

Wise God
You share your bread with strangers
And you welcome little children
AND YOU UNDERSTAND US

Wise God
You wrestle with the powerful
And you comfort all who need you
AND YOU DISTURB US

Wise God
Shining in darkness
Seen by those who love you
Found by those who seek you
WE ARE HERE TO LEARN FROM YOU

Kings and nations
Weak and powerful
ALL ARE COMING TO MEET WITH GOD

Sons and daughters
Rich and needy
ALL ARE COMING TO MEET WITH GOD

Strong and mighty
Weak and gentle

Star.
Moons
Sunshine
WE WILL WALK WITH GOD

Mountains
Main roads
Sidetracks
WE WILL WALK WITH GOD

Questions
Answers
Mysteries
WE WILL WALK WITH GOD

Backwards
Onwards
Homewards
WE WILL WALK WITH GOD

Ruth Burgess

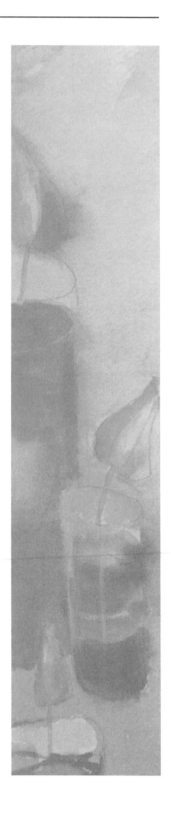

THE STRANGE COMING

Men rode rough,
by love of gain
saddled:
came frail Love
to take our part,
swaddled;

lies' proud rule
left our kind
befuddled:
came frail Truth
to light our life,
cuddled;

nations bent
on rapine, plunder,
pause:
their greed and fear
yield to
wonder.

Captive, bruised
and broken folk,
healing,
set the bells
of all the Earth
pealing.

Ian M Fraser

JOURNEYING WITH THE MAGI
A meditation

They set out to follow a star:
God is found in the moments of wonder that make us stop and ponder the mystery.
What have been your own 'awakening moments' of wonder that have led you deeper into mystery?

The star's light was seen in the darkness:
In their darker moments they trusted that the light was still to be found.
How have you experienced the dark? Where/how did you recognise the light?

They asked questions when they were lost:
Continuing to try to make sense of where they were and where they were being led, they looked for help.
What are the questions you live with?
Who are 'wisdom figures' for you? Who has helped you with your questions?

They travelled together:
We don't know how many of them, but we can imagine the little community that they became as they travelled together, sharing this experience.
Where do you experience community? What does this add to your journeying?

They met King Herod on the way:
For his own reasons of power and control he tried to deceive them. We need to recognise the twisted value systems of our world and not get caught up in them or be misled by them.
In what ways are you most often pulled off course?

They bowed down in adoration:

Falling on their knees they worshipped the King – a moment beyond intellectual understanding, and of recognition. We can imagine that moment of knowing in the deep silence.

Do you cultivate silence in your life so that there can be moments of knowing and of recognition?

They offered their gifts:

To be in the presence demanded a response, an offering – of themselves and of their gifts.

Identify your own gifts. What are you offering of yourself, your time and your material possessions?

In a dream they were shown the truth:

Because of the danger, they were warned to return by a different way.

Revelation can come to us through our dreams. Have you ever experienced this? How else do you experience God's revealing of the way to you?

For prayerful pondering:

Name and give thanks
for a moment of wonder.

Resolve to offer your gift this year
in a particular way.

Name some aspect of darkness
and pray for light.

Name a companion on the journey
and give thanks for their support.

Lynda Wright

(inspired by Michael Paul Gallagher's book Where is your God?*)*

FIELD MUSHROOMS

A glad epiphany.
We could see them from the first-floor window,
a surprise you could count upon,
boldly thrusting aside
the moist, red Somerset earth.
They sprang overnight into our perception,
with something slightly rude
about their pearly grey domes of pink.

We always knew they would be there
(though when was still uncertain).
Confidently we set off with our baskets,
the smallest basket for the smallest child,
and so on up.
We returned carefully
balanced over the stiles,
the mushrooms piled in great heaps
exposing their perfectly combed black underbellies,
which we were very careful not to bruise.

The kitchen scales announced prodigious harvests.
And then the tossing in hot butter
(our mother either knew not garlic or eschewed it)
and the mopping up the juices with good bread.

For many years – well into adulthood –
God could be similarly counted on
for an appearance.
Who moved? …
I swing from guilt to angry questioning,
but my cruel hide-and-seek companion never shows.

At times I am inclined to give up searching,
to settle for a mushroom-less menu.

But having tasted
I keep looking, waiting.
His hiddenness inspiring longing.

One day, I'll blink.
There'll be a pink bloom on the fields again.

Rosie Watson

CHRISTMAS GIFTS

Shining star! Jesus come.
Divine present for his mum.

Shepherds happy – cheers and shouts;
Joe, his father, has his doubts.

Pressies from the three wise sages;
Herod stamps his feet in rages.

All these actors play their part,
in a drama, in my heart.

Stuart Barrie

THE THREE KINGS

(*Tune: Personet Hodie*)

In the dark of the night
we have seen a strange sight
of a new star's bright light
calling us to follow,
leave our sleepy hollow.
    Moving out each day
    on the unknown way …
    from the old to the new,
    asking, looking, seeking.

O the nights are so cold
and our camels are old,
yet we go, brave and bold,
facing many dangers
through the lands of strangers.
    Moving out each day
    on the unknown way
    from the old to the new,
    asking, looking, seeking.

We have travelled so far
guided by our new star
to this byre door ajar.
Nothing could be stranger;
baby in a manger!
    Knowing from this day
    our new living way ...
    from the old to the new
    Love, in straw, lies sleeping.

Leith Fisher

EPIPHANY

Jesus,

may we not hoard,
but freely give

the gold of our hearts,
the myrrh of our grief,
the frankincense of our dreams,

to You.

Mary Palmer

THREE WISE MEN

It was Christmas in New York and Santa Claus had AIDS. The story was in all the papers. Macey's, the department store, had fired one of their in-house Father Christmases because he was HIV positive. I had gone there to do a freelance story for the newspapers based on the old theme of 'Christmas with the dossers in New York'.

When the job was finished, I told myself, I could go party with my pal David. Good old David, he's an amusing, dressy sort of guy in his early thirties, the sort you would ask to be a godfather to your children or to cheer up a dinner party where all the other guests were dull accountants. But it was a different David to the one I knew and loved who stumbled into the restaurant with his coat dirty and his demeanour sad.

He saw my expression and confirmed my fears before the waiter came to take our orders.

After his lover had died of AIDS, it had taken him four years to pluck up enough courage to have the test. Four years of checking his mouth in the mirror for sores and telling himself he was fine. Four years of good old David having three drinks before the party and as many as everyone else when he got there. Four years of a bottle by the bed for night frights, and one on the sideboard for day terrors, until he got himself together enough to have the test.

Now he was taking eight hundred dollars worth of medication a month including an 'alternative' one made from grass. This, he claimed, over coffee at his flat, was the one he had the most faith in. 'After all,' he laughed a little hysterically, 'who ever heard of a cow dying of AIDS?'

After coffee we ambled around Penn station and he told me that some surveys suggest that there may be up to two hundred thousand people in New York who are HIV positive. He said he personally knew of at least twenty people who had died in the previous year, and that every month friends would tell him of dozens of others. For gays, he said, it was rather like living through a war. He looked at me so sadly, and said, 'You know life's not really very funny any more.' It was Christmas in New York.

☆ ☆ ☆

I'm not sure whether I picked up John or he me.

It was 1 am on Christmas morning and I was standing in an all-night deli looking at a map and wondering if I dared walk down the street, let alone sleep on it.

'Can I help you, my friend?' said a voice that was alarmingly close. John was a six-foot wall of muscle and told me that he earned seventy thousand a year as a street shark who trawled the streets and offices broking clients for a house-letting agency, taking a few kick-backs here, a few there, and helping 'good folks when they was in trouble and the law won't help'.

His plan for Christmas night was to 'buy the bums off my conscience' by distributing a hamper of sandwiches to the homeless living in the street near his home. After hearing that I had planned to sleep with the homeless but was too scared, he suggested that we club together. By dawn we had given out over two hundred breakfasts. Most of the homeless we met were harmless drunks, but with them were the new homeless that told more about America in recession than any *Financial Times* article. The unemployed farm workers from the Midwest who slept with a clean shirt clutched to them in case they ever got an interview; the assembly line workers from Detroit who never slept; the big ladies; the AIDS victims; the inmates of New York institutions that a bankrupt city have deemed wise to 'return to the Community', without asking the Community if it

wanted them returned, because it already knew the answer.

Nobody knows how many homeless people there are in New York. Some say there are no more than ten thousand, some say no less than eight thousand, and yes, I'm talking about the city and not the state.

The end came with the dawn; it wasn't very pleasant. By then they were queuing and shouting for food and we simply ran out of breakfasts. John cried; the dossers swore; and I wished to heaven I had never come in the first place.

It was Christmas in New York.

☆ ☆ ☆

Then there was twenty-six-year-old Mark, the crack dealer.

He talked of women. He talked of drugs. He talked of clothes and of buying a Porsche.

He talked of smoking crack joints so close to his lips that the skin on his lips would blister; told of blowing seven hundred dollars in one weekend and then twelve hundred dollars the next, and not regretting a single moment of it. Then he boasted of all the 'hundreds' of women he had slept with and how he didn't know or care if he was HIV positive.

A young woman came up to us. She was probably about twenty but looked fifty and wore a scum-coated duffle coat. Her black hair was matted, her eyes streaming and there was a good deal of caked yellow mucus around her nose and blistered lips. Mark offered her his dreadful Yuletide greeting, and a bun.

She looked at him in horror.

'Don't you know me? Don't you know your honey? Don't you know the lady you lived with? Hey, come on, don't lay that on me.'

Visibly shaken, Mark went off for 'just a few private words'.

When he came back he said nothing at all.

It was Christmas in New York.

☆ ☆ ☆

I didn't submit any story about Christmas in New York. I tried to write it but couldn't.

I sat down and tried to write the story showing my three subjects as being three good men in New York at Christmas, each trying to make their own perverse systems of morality work in a city where to be moral at all was to be foolish.

'And the three wise men followed their stars until they came to the place where Jesus lay', perhaps?

Dream on.

It was Christmas in New York and Santa Claus had AIDS.

Maxwell MacLeod

LIGHT OF THE WORLD

(*Tune: Song 22, Orlando Gibbons (metre: 10.10.10.10)*)

Light of the world. Before all things were made,
when chaos reigned with empty darkness drear,
the Word was there, with God who spoke and said,
'Let all things come to be, let light appear.'

Light of the world. O'er Bethlehem's stable bare
see this strange star, this sign that day is near.
Look to this child, the light of God is there,
in Jesus Christ God's glory is made clear.

Light of the world. For nations near and far,
for wise and powerful folk, and those who bring
sad eyes and empty hands, yet seek the star;
all may bow low and find the earth's true king.

Light of the world. We hear this Jesus say,
I bring the light of hope and love and peace;
I call my friends to be my light today
to wait and serve and see the light increase.

Light of the world. Radiance of truth and love,
come, word made flesh, and make our hearts your home.
Come, Spirit come, come fire, come gentle dove,
to us, to all the world, come, quickly come.

Leith Fisher

MAGI

Magi, wise men
with the wisdom to know
that light comes by searching, by following;
and a touch of magical other-worldly majesty
in a simple manger.

All men, all folk
lacking wisdom
stumble around in the dark, in and out of the abyss,
hoping for light, hunting for angels,
for revelation,
looking everywhere but in the manger.

God
weeps grace over the world,
leading wise men on to glory,
offering all folk possibilities;
pours grace, pours out grace,
weak and despised, but beautiful.
Grace and glory in the manger.

I
struggle to be wise,
but I
get in the way,
and find myself in the dark
with everyone.
It's a long way up to God …
It's a long way down to the manger.

Carolyn Morris

BOWED PSALTERY MOMENTS, IONA 2000

Heading over to the MacLeod Centre for some fresh air and a quick bowl of soup – forcing myself out of my little office, narrow work-self, out of the head-down attitude that I must finish what I've started – and turning the corner, I see a woman in a gold lamé jacket and woollen hat with earflaps, playing some sort of stringed instrument in the sun. A bowed sultry, somebody says. 'A bowed what?' 'Psalter – as in psalm.' And we gather around the moment. I've never seen one before.

Triangular with silver strings – like a dulcimer, or an autoharp – the sound all silvery.

'*Ethereal* is the only way I can describe it,' the woman says, bowing obliquely – like some radiant angel.

She speaks with authority as a crowd gathers, her breath all spearminty: About how the bowed psaltery first came into being as an instrument at some point in the twelfth century, though there are some who believe it originated much earlier. And she plays us a song from Appalachia. Then a song she wrote about trees: About how there are no trees left where she comes from in Ohio. About how there are no trees left to touch and love and sit underneath. No trees left to give thanks to for cool shade, and branches sacrificed to make small, silvery-sounding instruments that give us life and remind us of heaven. No trees left to listen to singing in the gently strumming breezes. Just the sound of money everywhere. Silver money.

'Silver mon-ey,' she refrains and, reaching inside her jacket for another stick of chewing gum, tells us how the bowed psaltery made her come to Iona – to learn new tunes. Foil-wrap sparks and flashes, and just then Robbie from the hotel pulls up on his mountain bike and says he can't believe it – a bowed psaltery, his back wheels spinning with amazement. 'Never expected to find one here!' (He's gathered round with Anja, David, some more tourists, Abbey guests.) 'Probably not more than two bowed psalteries in all of Scotland,' he says. And he's got the other one, under his bed, back at The Columba. 'What are the odds of that?' he asks up at the gently smiling sky. 'One in a million,' and tears off on his bicycle, shooting stones and gravel that chime in his spokes; rides standing up, sailing and weaving in the wind.

'Ho-ly!' the woman sings out when he comes back with it tucked underneath his arm and lifts it carefully from a fantastically carved case.

He made the psaltery and the case himself, late nights, alone in his room, and they talk about tone woods – about how it doesn't matter what's on top, it's what's underneath that counts. They cradle and try out one another's psalteries. His is maple on bottom, piranha pine on top. He carved the rosette last thing.

'Far out.'

The bow's horsehair – he made that too.

Hers is ash, maple, some rosewood. There's a screech on her high E. 'See,' she bows, and giggles. 'She's got her own personality. No one's factory clone.'

'Sweet,' says Robbie, and they tune together to B flat. B flat. And just start suddenly playing. Jammin' psalteries on a smiling, sunny summer's day.

She plays some tunes first and he picks them up easily, watching her fingers; naturally, watching out at the waves – taps his sneakers in three/four, nodding his head, closing his eyes. Anja runs to grab her camera. (Anja, an artist at capturing moments: sunsets before they slide away into the sea, play of light and shadow, rainbows; moments like birds before they land and fold their wings – her vision born again on Iona.) Anja trying to capture now: the only two bowed psalteries in all of Scotland, meeting on a tiny island in the flow of time; crouching forward on her toes, back on her heels; holding her long hair aside like a curtain, like a veil. People stand smiling or with faraway expressions. Anja spins round silently – before they become aware, zoom back into themselves, lose their innocence, start hiding, posing. Lunch is getting cold. Work's piling up. I don't care, it doesn't matter. This moment is the reason for the whole day being. The sun feels good, warm, with me stopped in one place long enough for it to sink in; long enough to watch it glance off so it looks like sparks playing across silver strings. The day isn't dead any more; sparkles like the sun on the waves. I sketch poetry over an invoice. I'm not dead any more. A tourist starts singing. Just making stuff up. Closes her eyes. And isn't a tourist any more. People come and people leave with new in their eyes; drift back, filled with spirit, having as much fun as the players playing – folk songs, nursery rhymes, madrigals; melodies catchy and beautiful as laughter ringing. The crowd starts calling requests and the woman laughs out – glitteringly in rippling gold lamé. A child stands holding a balloon. Carnival red, pulling and tugging like a dog on a leash. There's a moment like something hanging and then shifting some place, and then Robbie starts showing the golden woman *Flower of Scotland*. Anja shifts and ducks, working to get inside the moment, inside the angle of the moment just perfect. They

play in unison. Then in harmony, perfect harmony. Then suddenly stop. And look at each other – the air all shivery with overtones. Like the meeting of heaven and earth for a flash: her golden jacket; his checked shirt, earthy shoes. When they finish everyone around claps out. Like light. There's a rainbow sheen in Anya's long, jet-black hair.

'Hey, that was a moment,' someone says. 'That was somethin', you know?'

'Yeah, it's not everyday, I guess.'

'Let's stay a bit longer.'

'Can't stay for ever.'

'One more song.'

'All right. Then catch the ferry back.'

When I leave, Robbie's showing her *The Leaving of Lismore. The Iona Boat Song*. People are still gathered around the moment. Like a beautiful sunset; but like watching it fade away after it's flowered, droop away into the sea, notes fading on the air. Like the last play of light and shadow as day resolves into evening.

I take a long lunch; walk back to work singing. There's a dance in my steps; a heavenly scent of mint past the herb garden with the rich earth all churned up. And I think: this is the challenge of these moments and meetings that jolt you back into life and all its fullness. To take the experience back into the everyday and not go to sleep again – Iona like one amazing moment I must take the experience of back into the everyday when I'm ready to leave; back onto the mainland. Back into 'the real world', as they say. The challenge: to see the wonder and miracle and beauty, and how God is working in moments there; to learn to sing a new song and go 'tell God's glory among all the nations. God's wondrous deeds to all the people'.

For these bowed psaltery moments must happen all the time, only we don't recognise them (pass them by like gardens); must annunciate themselves everywhere (for every place is holy) – every city corner, every traffic island – though in quieter, more subtle ways, perhaps. Different forms. Ways that demand a more practised eye, discipline, faith.

'Oh man,' I say to Robbie when I see him next day on the road.

'Yeah, jammin' psalteries,' he says, 'Well, long as people had fun, that's the main thing. See that kid with the balloon dancing?'

'Yeah, far out,' I sing, still drunk with it all, and gaze out at the sunlight, strumming across the sea.

'Sing to the Lord a new song …
Praise God's name with dancing,
making melody with tambourine and lyre.' (Psalm 149)

Neil Paynter

THE WISE MAN*

Now for the search.
We have played around for long enough
with all the theories about God,
pored over ancient manuscripts,
and studied ancient mysteries;
the time has come to venture all.

Leave behind the books and arguments,
the quiet days in shady cloisters,
and all the cleverness we have mutually admired.
Hardest of all we must say goodbye
to our reputation as 'wise men'.
We must now face the road, wherever it leads.

A blazing star, royal sign of Judah in the heavens,
crystallises all our thinking.
We must be fools to follow.
We will seek the face of God,
reach out for the ultimate mystery,
down the dusty road ahead.

Will fiery serpents bar our way?
Will there be cunning riddles to answer?
Will our path lead into the heart of fire?
Will it shrivel us to dust
when we finally see The Face?
No more questions. Saddle the camels.

… Months later …

Girths and saddles and bridles are not my trade.
Inns and stables sicken me.
Can this be the way?
Through raucous crowds of drunken camel drivers?
Oh please!
Not another inn!

Ian Cowie

* This poem reflects the popular, but probably inaccurate, picture of the wise men coming to the stable of an inn.

THE TRAVELLERS

It was the light that struck me first.
The jewelled sea
clear as the Aegean.

The panoply –
the depth of colour that heightened a profound experience
and left me tired.

My senses were bombarded:

Soft white sand.

Whipping winds
whistling round the abbey,
snuffing out the pew candles on dark mornings,
reminding us of our insignificance within nature.

Rocks that geologists came and tapped
with their little hammers –
Iona,
the third oldest piece of
land on Earth.

But more than this exotica were the people
who had followed their own stars.
Wise men and women who came from afar
and found a motley crew of fellow travellers
trying to discover the next stage of their journeys.

These pilgrims stayed a little while
and sang their songs
and delighted in each other's.

Travellers are rarely welcomed:
gypsies, asylum seekers, homeless folk, new age travellers,
people moving to a new town, disciples …
They sing different songs, new songs, fresh songs,
exciting and disturbing with their novelties.

Troubadour troupes that sing new harmonies
that echo in the memory
long after departure.

Pat Livingstone

GIVING

The weather is dismal and the Saturday papers likewise;
but life goes on, shopping goes on,
and I wait for early birds to approach me on this MS* flag day.
On they come, first in ones and twos, then in flocks:
weary women with bright-eyed bairns,
likely young lads in football shirts.
(I didn't think the boys would give, but they nudge each other and approach silently,
separately.)
Teenage girls in pastel pink giggle as they wait to give.
Women in smart suits search their handbags,
while casually dressed husbands chink coins in pockets helpfully.
'Oooh, your hands are freezing,' says one donor. 'Hope it doesn't rain. Good luck.'
An elderly man propped on a stick fumbles in his purse, his fingers swollen.
'Thank you, pet,' he says.
Thank you, thank you.
So many people say that as they give.
We share a moment's humanity and warmth on this cold morning.

Frances Copsey

* *Multiple sclerosis*

A LESSON IN HUMILITY

The wise men got it wrong.
It is *much* harder to receive
than to give.

Frances Copsey

WINTER BLESSING

When sleet blinds you,
hail drowns out voices,
and snow hides your path,

may you discern in each flake
a star, image of the one
that guided the Magi,

and find that in the pain
of birth, death or change

there is a light
to guide you.

Mary Palmer

FOLLOW THAT STAR

(*Tunes: Uttingen or Streets of Laredo*)

Once a small star led wise seekers to Bethlehem,
Now bright lights dazzle and lead us astray;
Worldlywise people, seduced by prosperity,
How can we hope to find Jesus today?

Seek out the family who circle their precious one,
Body or mind needing care night and day;
See the star shining where costly love's pouring out;
How can we hope to find Jesus today?

Turn to the neighbours who stand by the outcast one,
Labelled, rejected, with nowhere to stay;
See the star lighting the exiled one's homecoming;
How can we hope to find Jesus today?

Watch for the country that welcomes the stranger in,
Fleeing from hunger, from tyranny's sway;
See the star shine where the door's ever opening;
How can we hope to find Jesus today?

Mark where a nation renounces its weaponry,
Sharing wealth round to provide work and play;
See the star shine where the earth finds new cherishing;
How can we hope to find Jesus today?

Offer your gifts where the seeking ones yearn for them,
Welcome the love which they more than repay;
Healing comes swiftly where human hearts turn again;
Turn to the star and find Jesus today.

Anna Briggs

THE PROFESSOR

From a longer story about working in a home for people with mental health challenges

The professor was once a doctor of psychology, ten years ago or so, someone said. I don't know what happened to the professor. Some people carry so much weight around with them that it is inevitable they collapse under it all.

We pass his room on our rounds to recruit bingo players. It's hard to give a complete picture: broken chairs and tables; a cracked full-length mirror reflecting a thousand different perspectives; food welded on paper plates; heaps of clothes like mountain ranges; a hundred books of different sizes and subjects scattered north, south, east, west, in different regions of the landscape, in various stages of being read and not read; and faded orange-brown pine needles and earth sprinkled over the entire expanse of the room – from the three small, dead evergreen trees the professor, nevertheless, stubbornly, faithfully replants from flower pot to flower pot: like a scientist pouring from test tube to test tube; like an alchemist searching for the mythical, mystical reaction.

It's as if, after the bomb was dropped, the professor believed himself to be the only survivor left on earth, and to be charged with the enormous, profound responsibility of salvaging and reordering the world.

And the earth was without form and void.

He sits cross-legged like a monk — he's shaved his head — in the midst of the rubble of his darkened room, amongst the remains of the silent world, and moves his trembling hand over the landscape.

And the spirit of God moved upon the face of the waters.

Then, he suddenly acts. He picks up *this* and places it there, there, at a precise angle, within degrees, as if it must be positioned just so in order to receive certain vibrations and signals which run up through it and into the receptive professor. He lifts up *that* and sets it down way over there, no, way over here. On the way the professor trips over a teapot, upsetting the order of the world ... The professor scratches his chin. The professor scratches his head. He sits down beside an empty bookcase, which stands like a central monolith, contemplating its tall, smooth back, as he waits to be pregnant with inspiration again...

There was a period of about three weeks when we never saw the professor working in his room. Then, one evening, he appeared in the basement for Bingo! He'd never come down before, had never spoken to us, or recognised us, I thought. I was surprised. It was good to see him. 'Hallo,' I said.

'I won't win, he answered, 'but I came down to be around people.'

Later, we discovered he'd been in the hospital for the three weeks we hadn't seen him. One night at the rest home he ate a tube of glue. Maybe the despair of not being able to reorder the world had finally got to him; or it was a last, desperate act. But glue is not strong enough to hold the world, or yourself, together, from falling into ragged pieces. One never knows, it may have been an accident; maybe the professor thought it was toothpaste or God knows what. The professor was rushed to hospital and pumped out, then shocked into sense with ECT.

Now, John plays Bingo with us every week. Getting five in a row or even four corners is a much simpler order.

The staff said, 'Let there be light', and there was light. They pulled open his heavy drapes and let the face of the real world in; blitzed and gutted his bedroom. It took some time but they gave it the established order. (Since then, John has developed a neatness fetish. He is obsessive. His room is immaculate; maybe he fears having to fight Chaos again.)

Everyone tells him that he's doing so much better. I say it too.

But it's sad, in a way, seeing the professor's room like everyone else's. Sad, in a way, seeing the humbled professor meekly following the established order, waiting in line at medication times, hair grown back, combed neat. The professor: another cowed old man playing Bingo and winning soda pop. The professor, John, aging now.

Neil Paynter

UNTIL THE NEEDLES DROPPED

During my boyhood,
in a German-American neighbourhood
in the depression of the 1930s,
Christmas trees were not decorated until Christmas Eve.

As the youngest child of four siblings,
I was led to believe
that Santa not only brought presents on Christmas Eve
but also brought the tree and decorated it!

I would be taken to a movie in the afternoon,
about a mile from home.

Later,
walking homewards in the darkening evening,
we would loiter,
counting the houses where trees were lit,
seeing where Santa had already come.

Every once in a while
my older sister would go to a public telephone;
I knew not why.

Finally home –
Santa had come.
The tree brightened our drab living room
for many days,
remaining until its needles had dropped.

Sad was the day
when I returned from school
and it had vanished.
Its departure bringing to an end
the lingering, tender and simple joys of Christmas.

Ed Daub

BAPTISM OF JESUS

Lectionary readings
Isaiah 42:1–4,6–7; Psalm 29; Acts 10: 34–38

Year A:
Matthew 3:13–17

Year B:
Mark 1:7–11

Year C:
Luke 3:15–16,21–22

RESPONSES

Mountains and rivers
Islands and oceans
GIVE GOD GLORY

Children and lovers
Rulers and nations
GIVE GOD GLORY

All who live
All who breathe
GIVE GOD GLORY

> Exciting God
> Glorious God
> BAPTISE US WITH WONDER

> Wise God
> Righteous God
> BAPTISE US WITH JUSTICE

> Holy God
> Covenant God
> BAPTISE US WITH LOVE

Ruth Burgess

FATHER TO SON

Luke 1:67–80 (The Benedictus, sung or read)

John:	Dad, was I ever baptised?
	(Pause)
	Dad!
Zechariah:	Urr … *(rousing himself)* … I'm sorry, I was just thinking of something else. Did you say something John?
John:	I was wondering whether I was baptised when I was a baby – now that mother's died there are so many things that I realise I never asked her.
Zechariah:	No, not baptised, but you were done on the eighth day. Oh, that was quite a day … quite a day …
John:	What do you mean?
Zechariah:	You know what they were going to call you?
John:	Yes, you told me that. Zechariah Junior. I was to be named after you.
Zechariah:	They wouldn't listen to your mother, you know; it was only when I wrote it down for them that they gave in.
John:	And then you got your voice back, didn't you?
Zechariah:	Umm … *(thinking, remembering)*
John:	Dad, you know that thing you wrote out for me on my thirteenth birthday? Where did you get that?
Zechariah:	Well, it sort of came to me during all that time when I couldn't talk. People began to assume that I couldn't hear as well. To be honest, they thought I'd gone mad I think. So people left me alone.
John:	Was that all that 'came to you'?
Zechariah:	Yes … well, almost … there was a bit more I never wrote down for you.

John:	*(excitedly)* Really, what else was there about me?
Zechariah:	Oh, it wasn't about you, that's why I never wrote it down.
John:	Oh *(disappointed)* … Who was it about then?
Zechariah:	I don't know. Well, that's to say I do know *what* it was about, but not *who*.
John:	What?
Zechariah:	It was about the Lord's anointed one for whom I believe you are preparing the way.
	(Pause)
John:	Preparing the way. Dad, you believe in me, don't you? *You* don't think I'm mad, do you?
Zechariah:	No, son, I don't. Just because people think you're mad, it doesn't mean you are – believe you me. I know the path you have chosen is a hard one, but it's the right one, you know?
	(Silence)
	Son, is there something bothering you?
John:	Well, it's just this funny thing that happened today. I was out by the river, as you know, as I've been all week. Just as the sun was at its highest, this guy came along to be baptised. I just felt I knew him somehow, and there was a sort of light in his eyes as if he knew me too. It was strange. The sun so bright on the water. People suddenly went quiet … You know, I think he is the one.
	(Pause)
	Dad, are you listening to me?
Zechariah:	Urr … *(rousing himself)* … I'm sorry, I was just thinking of someone else. I was thinking of your mother. She would know.

Richard Sharples

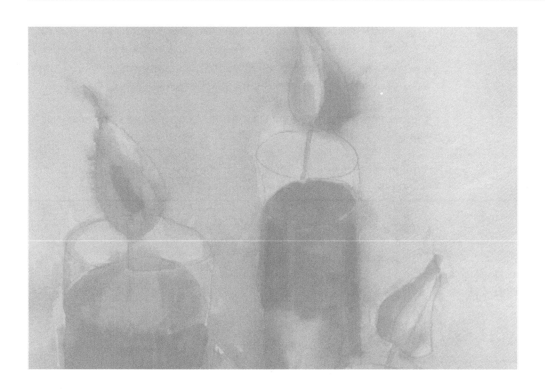

MOTHER TO SON

Luke 1:46–56 (The Magnificat, sung or read)

Jesus: Mum, was I ever baptised?

             (Pause)

             (Gently) Mum, are you all right?

Mary: Oh, I'm sorry, love, I'm not quite all here. What was that you said?

Jesus: Mum, you can hardly expect to carry on at your usual pace – it's only three months since father died, you know.

Mary: Oh, I know all right. *(Pause)* What were you asking?

Jesus: I was wondering what you had done for me when I was a baby; I mean, I realise my birth was a little embarrassing for the family.

Mary:	Jesus, a little embarrassment has never bothered your father and me. We had you done when you were eight days old just like everybody else. We even took you along with us to the temple for my purification a few weeks later. That was quite a day ... quite a day ...
Jesus:	I know the old lady was called Anna, but what was the old man's name?
Mary:	Simeon; but they just confirmed for me what I had known all along. 'This child,' Simeon said, 'is chosen by God for the destruction and the salvation of many in Israel. He will be a sign from God which many people will speak against, and so reveal their secret thoughts.'
Jesus:	Do you believe that, mum?
Mary:	I do. One day, through you, this world is going to be turned upside down.

(Pause)

Jesus, what are you thinking?

Jesus:	I'm thinking that the time has come. I don't think I'll be around home for much longer; I feel I need to be 'about my Father's business'. (*Laughing*) You remember how I told you that, mum, when I was all of thirteen years old? But now I really do. I see so much suffering around. And the injustice of this occupation, and of so-called religion, just makes me angry. But I don't need to convince you, do I? That thing you wrote down for me on my thirteenth birthday said it all.

(Pause)

Mum, did the old man say anything else?

Mary:	... Not about you.
Jesus:	Go on.
Mary:	I've never told you this: He said that a sword will pierce my soul, too – and when you were talking just now, I felt that it did.

Jesus: I want you to know, mum, that I was baptised today by John.

                  (Pause)

                  Mum, did you hear what I just said?

Mary: Yes, Jesus, I did. I was just thinking of your father. He would be so proud of you.

Richard Sharples

TURN US AROUND

Turn us around, God –
around into your way of thinking,
around into your way of loving.

Turn us around, God,
and confront us with Jesus.
Baptise our fears with your joy.

Ruth Burgess

CHRISTIAN UNITY

YOUR BODY, THE CHURCH

We ask you to
forgive the sin that mingles
even with our holiest actions.

Forgive us for the ways in which
we have hurt and dismembered
your body, the church.

Forgive us for any way in which
we have, thoughtlessly or deliberately,
insulted or patronised
those who are called by the same name as ourselves.

Forgive us if we have prayed for unity
and done nothing,
or very little,
to help bring it about,
preferring prayers to action
and fantasies to hard reality.

Be active,
be disturbing,
be empowering,
in your church,
and among Christian people throughout the world.

Remind us of the mighty company
in heaven and on earth
to which we all belong.

John Harvey

HAVE MERCY ON YOUR CHURCH

Lord God,
whose son was content to die
to bring new life,
have mercy on your church
which will do anything you ask,
anything at all,
except die
and be reborn.

Lord Christ,
forbid us unity
which leaves us where we are
and as we are:
welded into one company
but extracted from the battle;
engaged to be yours,
but not found at your side.

Holy Spirit of God,
reach deeper than our inertia and fears:
release us into the freedom of children of God.

Ian M Fraser

Note: *The Week of Prayer for Christian Unity usually takes place from the 18th/25th of January.*

GOD OF MANY NAMES

God of many names,
revealed and hidden,
we welcome You
in our midst.
Bring to our lives
the oil of justice,
the lamp of truth.

Strengthen us as we meet
in fellowship and doubt.
Guard us with Your cherishing embrace.

Challenge us as we engage
in dialogue and debate,
provoking us to undermine
walls of division between us.

Remind us to listen
more than we speak;
to be open to receive
more than we can give.

Inspire us on the journey
with the vision of Christ's passion
to bring light to the world
and glad hearts to those in mourning.

As we wait for the breath
of the Spirit to fill us,
keep us ever ready to prophesy,
to see visions and to dream dreams.

As we rejoice in the tasks
which are before us,
walk beside us through our darkness
so that, in You, we will not fail.

Yvonne Morland

HOMELESSNESS SUNDAY

I NEVER KNEW HIS NAME

I never knew his name;
but each day I walked past
on my way from work;
he was there, in the doorway,
huddled with his old dog.

Sometimes I gave him my apple
left over from lunch,
and felt good because I'd given up
a tiny morsel of a meal
when I had so much.

And if I did, he smiled up at me
through the scruffy growth of his beard,
and the dog tried to wag its tired tail
as it chewed on scraps thrown out
by benevolent butchers.

One day he wasn't there and I heard
he'd been found dead that morning
after a particularly cold night.
The dog was taken into a shelter.
On a string round its neck,
he'd hung its name, Fido – 'Faithful'.

And his name?
From a paper in his pocket
it seems his name was Josh,
short for Joshua –
another name for Jesus.

A prayer

Lord God,
how kind we are to animals –
they are so easy to deal with.
They don't ask awkward questions
or demand more of us
than we are prepared to give.

But when it comes to human beings,
created in your own image,
often we turn away, unable to cope
with facing up to others' needs,
even if, in so doing, we are rejecting you.

Help us to know how we can help the homeless
to help themselves, preserving their dignity,
giving them hope, for the sake of Jesus, your son,
who brought us home, into your kingdom
where all are accepted and loved.

Carol Dixon

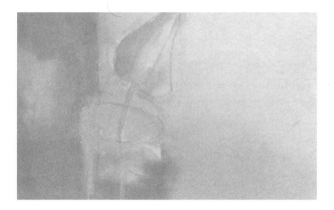

TWO VOICES

The first thing
they ask you is
'Where do you live?'
Giro, job application, bank account –
you need an address.
'No fixed abode'
conjures up a shifty kind of person –
likely to move on
but with nowhere to go –
neither credit-worthy
nor credible.

The last thing
I'd want is for bricks and mortar
to come between me
and what God
might be calling me to do.
But I have a mortgage.
That makes me a solid citizen.
Credit-worthy, credible,
a good neighbour –
behind my own front door –
most likely to stay put.
In fact, I'd find it hard to move.

The last thing I think of
when you say 'home' is comforts –
they come later.
First it has to become
more than a memory or a fantasy.
It has to become something real and present:
Home being 'where the heart is' rings hollow.

The first thing I think of
when you say 'home' is insurance –
and then I remember
that failure to keep up mortgage repayments
could result in the repossession of my home.
My commitments lay a dead hand on my heart.

God, whose home is the whole world
and who became homeless for our sake;
Creator of the universe,
who put us on earth as housekeepers,
whose care for all that is made
embraces ecosystems and economies;
who came to share our lives:
born on a travellers' site,
becoming a refugee;
growing up in a nuclear family,
learning a trade;
leaving home and encouraging solid citizens to drop out,
wandering from place to place,

always having time for folk on the margins;
  disappointing your family,
  but enjoying the welcome of ordinary homes and shared meals;
having nowhere to lay your head;
  welcomed into the city;
disrupting the house of God;
  gathering your friends in a strange room;
arrested as an anti-social element;
  put to death on the town dump;
buried in a borrowed grave.

We rejoice that you rose again,
overcoming the death that we all fear,
  death of the spirit as well as the body.
We give thanks that you remind us
  that all people matter
  and that new life is possible.
We need your help to rise beyond our own insecurity –
  and too great security.
We believe that in you is our real and eternal home
  for you are Alpha and Omega
the first and last.
Amen

Jan Sutch Pickard

CANDLEMAS

THOUGHTS AND PRAYERS FOR CANDLEMAS

Candlemas is celebrated as a winter festival of birth and light. It is also a story of living, ageing and learning. The wisdom of age, the years of struggling and hurting and loving, the presenting of themselves regularly in the communal round of worship, the prayers of a lifetime – these are the experiences that enable Simeon and Anna to recognise God in Jesus and to have confidence in the safety and vulnerability of God's love.

> Like Simeon,
> may I grow old
> in hope and in wonder.
>
> Like Anna,
> may I be in love with you
> all my days.
>
> May I be open to truth,
> open to surprises.
>
> May I let your Spirit
> into my life.
>
> May I let your justice
> change my behaviour.
>
> May I live in the brightness
> of your joy.

Living and dying, striving for holiness and justice, accepting forgiveness and affirmation, living with the questions and the mystery, trusting in hope of home and the glory and the light of resurrection – these are the elements of life and loving that dance and burn in the candles of Candlemas. And these are the candles that are offered to us so that, lit by God's bright fire, we may be light and warmth for God's world.

> Starmaker God,
> Lightener of the world,
> bless us
> and warm us
> into light and loving.
> Bring us to the light of Jesus
> all the length and breadth
> of our nights and days.

You have found me.
I have seen you.
Daily I know you
cherishing me.

Kindle and draw me
into the light of your loving
every night and day
of my journey home.

As the candle,
so my life;
flickering, burning, changing,
alight and warm
with the light
which is you.

Ruth Burgess

AN OLD SAINT FOR NEW WAYS

A story and a play for a Candlemas service

Some biographical information about Saint Brigit should be given before reading the story. After listening to the story, folk could be asked to think of a creative project they might wish to pursue in the next year. If asked this question before the day/evening of the service, they could bring in a project they are working on, an idea …

The story

St Brigit climbed down from her horse and stretched her aching limbs. She glanced around for Sister Catherine who had been with her. Where on earth was the silly girl? As always, she had rushed ahead, ever anxious to know what would be happening tomorrow, before she rightly knew what was happening today. And now she was nowhere to be seen. The horse, meanwhile, was quite content to stop. He wandered to the side of the road to crop the new-grown grass. Brigit looked at him. So many creatures had been associated with her over the course of time: sheep with their newborn lambs; owls; clumsy, quacking ducks; a little white heifer with red ears. They had been company for her over the years; but no one had ever thought to mention her old horse who trotted amiably through the centuries with her, carrying her, without fail, on the eve of every Candlemas, from holy place to holy place. He was a little stiff with age now, as indeed was she. Still, that was hardly surprising; they had both been around for such a long time. Sixteen hundred years at least, though it could be more, she couldn't really remember. Sixteen hundred years of travelling to so many different places and countries. It was no wonder they were both becoming a little the worse for wear.

She looked at the church she was coming to visit now. She knew so many places like this, though they didn't always recognise her. Such places seemed perhaps rather tired and old, but yet, in their grey, quiet steadiness, they also seemed somehow rooted in the landscape. And from roots could spring new growth. And she, coming in the spring as she always did, was the saint to bring just that! She opened the gate to the churchyard. It creaked. She smiled to herself. That was what she felt like – a creaking gate. The gate opened onto a path. She walked along it.

In a corner of the churchyard, two men were trying to light a bonfire. They had gathered all the old wood brought down by the winter gales, the dead flowers from the graves and all the remaining leaves from the previous autumn. But the heap of rubbish was damp and resistant and didn't want to be set on fire. The men were trying hard, but were cold and tired now, after all their work, and were becoming grumpy with one another. Brigit smiled, approving of their efforts; she was glad they were trying. Now they just needed a little help from her. Raising her hand, she threw sparks of fire from the ends of her fingertips. The bonfire blazed up and the men jumped back in surprise. Well, what was the point of being a saint if you couldn't work the odd miracle or two? And was not this Candlemas, the time of purifying fire? It was so important to clear away the rubbish, in order that the new growth could begin.

Fire, she thought. People had always associated her with fire. Did not her very name mean 'fiery arrow'? She remembered the day when she and her fellow sisters had been about to be received into the monastic life. She had been standing at the end of the line but the bishop, who was to confirm them all, called her to the front. He had seen that a fiery pillar rose from her head to the roof of the church and recognised that she had already become a temple of the Holy Spirit. He received her, therefore, not as a nun, but with the ordination prayer for a bishop. Those around him were shocked; but he replied: 'I do not have any power in this matter. That dignity has been given by God to Brigit.'

Brigit smiled, remembering. Luckily, she was not one to stand on dignity! She remembered also how someone had written that 'her heart and mind were a throne of rest for the Holy Spirit'. Well, thank goodness the Holy Spirit had somewhere to rest, she thought, given the amount of work She had to do!

She came to the church door and turned the handle. It was open. Good. That was

something. She didn't like it when the door was locked against anyone who might want to come in. Oh, she understood the fear, of course she understood it. Had not her own shrine at Kildare, where her light had been tended so faithfully for over a thousand years, been damaged and destroyed. And that had been not by a casual thief or a bored vandal, but by those who felt it was right she should be destroyed. Who was she to say they were wrong? Flames needed to wax and wane, to change their form from time to time; and anyway, they had not succeeded in destroying her. As if the mere extinguishing of an outer light could affect the shining of an inner light.

She walked into the church. Somewhat dark perhaps, a little dusty and tired, rather cold. But light and warmth could still come through the windows, brightening the shapes of the saints and angels so that they would fall, colour-dappled, across the congregation. And there, in the Lady Chapel, was a small, bright light, showing the presence of the reserved sacrament, symbol of the one true Light that could never be put out and which, although tiny, was capable of filling the whole world with itself. And there at the front of the church were candles for each member of the congregation, ready for Candlemas. Candles to be lit as a reminder that the infant Christ was brought, 2000 years ago, to the temple and there recognised as the Light of Revelation.

So really, all that was necessary was here.

She walked down the aisle of the church and gently picked up the candles, one by one. She remembered her monastery at Kildare. It had become a centre of learning. There had been art and poetry, craftwork and writing. There had been a copy of the gospels made with such beautiful illuminations and harmonies of colours that it had been called the work of angels. There had been healing. She knew great healing could come through creativity. She turned the candles in her hands. As each member of this community here lit their candle for Christ, she wanted them also to think of the creativity which was within them; creativity which they had perhaps ignored, or dismissed, or simply not recognised; creativity which was perhaps a little dark and dusty, a little tired, rather cold, but which had yet within it a small bright light of the one true Light, and which was waiting to grow within them. Some song, some poem, some drawing, some dance, some tapestry, some sculpture, some music, which was entirely and uniquely their own and which, as yet, they had not developed. She wanted them to acknowledge that gift in themselves, however big or small it might be, and promise to develop it in the coming year as part of their dedication and service to Christ.

She moved on to the Lady Chapel. There was a statue of Mary, her sister in Christ, holding the infant Jesus in her arms. Brigit remembered herself as mother. There was a legend that she had been the wet nurse of Christ, that she had nourished him with her own milk. She remembered also a tale of when she had received seven bishops and had had nothing to feed them. She had prayed for help and angels had appeared, telling her to milk the cows for the third time that day. When she did so, all the pails were filled and there was enough left over to create an entire lake! If you prayed, there was always enough and more. This is what she wished for the people here: that they might be so overflowing with the milk of human kindness that they, too, would have plenty and a lake to spare.

Brigit moved away to the door and looked back at the church. There was blessing here, she thought; the blessing of people and their gifts, the blessing of spring and new beginnings and, above all, the blessing of Christ.

She walked out into the churchyard. The bonfire had died down now and the men were raking over the ashes. As Brigit walked past them, silent and unseen, her cloak touched the earth and the flowers of spring burst through – snowdrops, aconites, violas … Brigit smiled. She felt young again, a maiden in the spring.

Suddenly, she heard a voice calling her, loudly, anxiously.

'Oh, St. Brigit, Mother, where are you? Something terrible has happened! Whatever are we going to do?'

She sighed. Sister Catherine. What had she been up to? Well, she was clearly just about to find out, for here the girl was, rushing up the path, waving a newspaper.

The play

This short play is designed to be acted out in a parish church but can be easily adapted to suit any worship space. The play could take the place of a sermon.

At the centre, in front, a large candleholder is in place. There is a sturdy chair placed stage right, with a footstool beside it. There is also a box of small candles, sufficient for each member of the congregation, set to one side. St Brigit, dressed as a nun and carrying a large white candle, enters through the church door at the back. She is a benign, steady character, in late middle age. A motherly sort. She is accompanied by Sister Catherine, a young fellow nun. The latter is brandishing a newspaper and is clearly agitated. St Brigit is trying to calm her down.

St Brigit:	*(making her way down the aisle)* Sister Catherine, you've been getting yourself in a state again. You rush on ahead of me, so I don't know where you are or what you're doing. And then you come back all upset.
Sister Catherine:	Yes, Mother, I just went to get a newspaper.
St Brigit:	All this dashing around really doesn't do you any good, you know. If you could just calm down and help me to help these good people celebrate Candlemas.
Sister Catherine:	*(jabbing at the newspaper)* But Mother, look at this. They're going to be doing the most terrible things to you!
St Brigit:	*(completely unconcerned)* Are they dear? How dreadful! *(By now, they have reached the front of the church. St Brigit sits down heavily and puts her feet up on the footstool with a sigh of relief. She sets down her candle and reaches out for the newspaper.)* Here, let me have a look. Ah, 'The News in Future'. Is that what's upsetting you? Where are we now, my dear? The past or the present? I'm never too sure. *(She hands back the paper.)* In any case, my dear, I shouldn't bother yourself too much. 'Take no thought for the morrow', you know, and 'Sufficient unto the day is the evil thereof'. *(Sister Catherine is still obviously distressed.)* Still, as you've got yourself so agitated, you'd better tell me all about it and relieve your feelings.
Sister Catherine:	*(consulting the newspaper, agonised)* It says here that they're not going to let you be a saint any longer. You're going to be decanonised!

St Brigit:	Oh, is that all? I thought it was going to be something important.
Sister Catherine:	Being decanonised! Not important!
St Brigit:	My dear girl, do you think I mind in the slightest whether I am a saint or not? My job is just to get on with what I'm supposed to be doing. Don't worry about it.
Sister Catherine:	But, Mother, you don't understand. You're going to be fired!
St Brigit:	Fired! Yes, well indeed I am fired. Fired with enthusiasm, fired with life, fired with the Holy Spirit, so they say. *(She gets to her feet, picks up the candle and places it in the candleholder.)* And, principally – as I hope we all are – fired with the Light of Christ.
Sister Catherine:	Yes, yes, Mother, I know but –
St Brigit:	*(interrupting her)* Let us remember what we are all here for: *(Gospel reading – Luke 2:22–40. At the end of the reading, St Brigit moves to the large candle.)* So here we have it. The Light of Christ. Shining in his temple … *(After a short pause, Sister Catherine moves to the box of small candles.)*
Sister Catherine:	*(picking up one or two of the candles)* What are these for?
St Brigit:	Ah, this is where I come in. This is the exciting bit. As you know, Sister Catherine, I am a saint associated with learning, with poetry and writing, with art and all manner of craftsmanship. I'm known for my generosity to all in need. I am a saint of healing, and I know that great healing comes through those twin gifts of creativity and generosity. Coming at this time of the year as I do, with my day on the 2nd of February, I inspire and invite people to light the candle of their creativity and capacity to care, in the light of Christ, and to commit themselves, in the year coming, to developing and unfolding those gifts.
Sister Catherine:	Goodness. Do you think they'll do it?
St Brigit:	Oh, I think so. *(Looks around the church)* They look a reasonable lot. They just need the opportunity. We'll give them a little while to think about it. Now *(to the congregation. The following is only a suggested speech.)* I want you to think about something creative that you would like to do in the next year. It can be anything.

Something you want to do – some painting, some poem, some writing, some sewing, some reading, some sculpture, some dance, some caring, something which you know is within you, but which perhaps, for all sorts of reasons, you have shut out of your hearts for far too long. Think about it. What comes to mind? What new seeds will you grow in the new year? *(A time of reflective silence follows.)*

Lighting candles

(After the time of silence, people are invited to come to the front and to light a candle as a symbol of their creative intention for the year. St Brigit and Sister Catherine hand out the candles.)

St Brigit:	At Christmas, we all received the Christ child into our hearts. We saw Him and knew Him. Now He is brought to the temple and we recognise him anew and see how he is growing within us. We recognise the creative power of Christ within us. We recognise the caring power of Christ within us. We bring His Light to our light and let new seeds grow, new shoots in our new year.

Song or poem

St Brigit:	There, that's done. It all looks a bit brighter in here now, doesn't it? Excellent. Now come along, Sister Catherine. We have to be off. *(To the congregation)* It's been very nice to meet you all. I hope you have a wonderfully creative and fulfilling year, all thoroughly blessed in the Light of Christ.
	(She begins to walk down the aisle. Sister Catherine starts after her, snatching up the newspaper as she goes.)
Sister Catherine:	Yes, Mother, all that's all very well, but it also says here that there is considerable doubt about whether you ever really existed!
St Brigit:	*(comfortably, over her shoulder)* Oh well, if I don't exist, then they can't decanonise me, can they?
Sister Catherine:	*(can't quite get her head round this)* What?!
St Brigit:	Oh, never mind, dear, never mind. You'll understand when you're older. Maybe. In the meantime, it's important to remember that the message is far more important than the messenger.

Sister Catherine: Oh, yes Mother, I suppose so. But then there's this bit. It says you're actually a pagan goddess!

St Brigit: Goodness! Was that before or after I failed to exist?

Sister Catherine: *(wailing despairingly)* Mother! Why can't you take me seriously?

St Brigit: Because it isn't necessary to take you seriously. It doesn't help you or me. All you really need to know is that there is much living truth to be found in the stories of the saints, whether those stories are mythical or actual. And the living truth is what it's all about. And, hopefully, that's what all these good people here are in the process of finding, through their creativity and their caring for one another. Now come along, dear. There are an awful lot of other places we need to visit before the end of the day.

Sister Catherine: Coming Mother, coming.

     (She follows St Brigit down the aisle to the back door.)

St Brigit: *(as they go out)* And for goodness sake put that paper in the bin before we go anywhere else. No, on second thought, put it in the recycling.

Alison Pearson

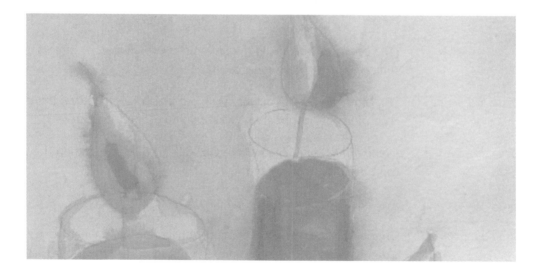

BENEDICTUS

(Tune: Bunessan (Morning has broken))

Blessed be God
For he has redeemed us,
Given us a saviour,
David's great Son;
Tell out his praise,
Sing in thanksgiving,
From all our foes
Our freedom is won.

Prophets foretold
That he'd come with mercy,
Keeping his promise
Made through the years,
Bringing deliverance
From all who'd harmed us;
Joyfully serve him,
Free from all fears.

To those in darkness
God's sun has risen,
His tender mercy
Bringing us light,
Taking away
The dread of death's shadow,
Guiding us onward
Out of the night.

Praise to the Father,
praise to the Spirit,
Praise to the Son,
Christ Jesus our Lord;
From the beginning,
Now and for ever
May you be worshipped,
Praised and adored.

Margaret Harvey

CLOSING RESPONSES

As Anna and Simeon recognised you in the temple
MAY WE RECOGNISE YOU IN THOSE WE MEET

As Brigit kept your light shining in times of darkness
MAY WE BE LIGHT FOR THOSE IN NEED

As Jesus grew and became strong and wise
MAY WE GROW IN WISDOM AND WONDER AND JOY. AMEN

Ruth Burgess

CANDLEMAS

I do not believe Mary needed purification after Jesus was born.
Or, millennia later, that my own mother required 'churching' when she bore me.
But Candlemas is such a sweet feast,
so redolent of hope when spring first stirs in the dark land,
that I cannot spare it.
We are messy creatures from our birth to death I know,
I know.
Even so the snowdrop spears up through the dank soil
immaculate in its purity.

Frances Copsey

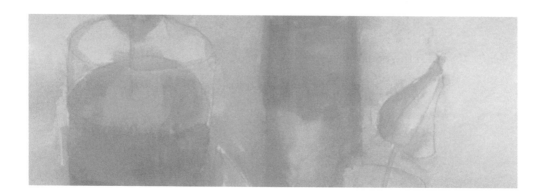

CELEBRATING OLD AGE

Abraham and Sarah
celebrated old age
by selling up and going travelling
OLDER PEOPLE ARE LED BY GOD

Sarah and Tobit
celebrated old age
by loving and growing closer together
OLDER PEOPLE ARE BLESSED BY GOD

Anna and Simeon
celebrated old age
by discovering what they'd yearned for
OLDER PEOPLE ARE GIFTED BY GOD

God says, 'In your old age I will take care of you.
When your hair is grey,
I will give you help and support.'*
OLDER PEOPLE ARE CHERISHED BY GOD.

Ruth Burgess

* Isaiah 46:4

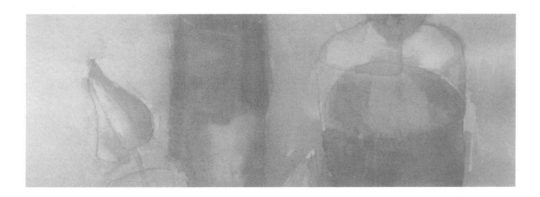

A FLAME THAT CANNOT BE PUT OUT

In the dark days:
under rain-heavy clouds,
among broken branches,
on sodden earth,
the snowdrops light their candles.

A flame that cannot be put out
by darkness or gales or doubt.

In the salt wind,
rooks buckle like broken umbrellas;
as the bare trees
heave a great sigh,
the snowdrops tremble.

But their flame cannot be put out
by darkness or gales or doubt.

Perfect, as though carved
in green-veined marble,
life pulsing through tissue
delicate as the eyelids
of a sleeping child,
curved like small fingers, holding on.

Their flame is steadfast:
it is full of hope and new beginnings.
Darkness or gales or doubt
cannot put it out.

Jan Sutch Pickard

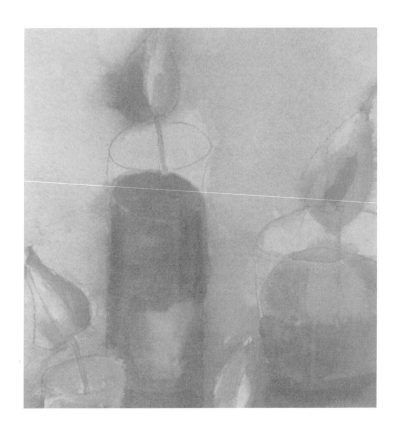

SOURCES AND ACKNOWLEDGEMENTS

Every effort has been made to trace copyright holders of all the items reproduced in this book. We would be glad to hear from anyone whom we have been unable to contact so that any omissions can be rectified in future editions.

'Christmas seen' – by Stuart Barrie, first published in *Coracle*, the magazine of the Iona Community, autumn 1989. Coracle: ionacomm@gla.iona.org.uk

'Stay my child' – Daniel Charles Damon/Anna Briggs, Copyright © 1992 Hope Publishing Company, administered by Copycare, P.O. Box 77, Hailsham BN27 3EF UK music@copycare.com Used by permission.

'Hush! Watch! Hear!' – words by Ian M Fraser © 1994 Stainer & Bell Ltd. Music (Breath-holding carol) – tune by Ian M Fraser, arranged by Donald Rennie © 1994 Stainer & Bell Ltd.

Isaac's carol – Words © Isaac Hutchings; music © 2003, Wild Goose Resource Group, Iona Community, Glasgow G2 3DH, Scotland.

'Prayer at Christmas' – by Jill Rhodes, first published in *Coracle,* the magazine of the Iona Community, December 2000. ionacomm@gla.iona.org.uk

'Sometimes I cry' © Kathy Galloway, first published in *Love Burning Deep: Poems and lyrics,* p 32, SPCK, 1993, ISBN 0281046425 (out of print). Used by permission of Kathy Galloway.

Bethlehem 2002 – first published in *Coracle,* the magazine of the Iona Community ionacomm@gla.iona.org.uk

Your child's coming was my child's going – words by Ian M Fraser © 1994 Stainer & Bell Ltd. Music (Rachel weeping) – tune by Ian M Fraser, arranged by Nicholas Williams © 1994 Stainer & Bell Ltd.

'Step softly' – by Carol Dixon, first published on the Northern Synod website.

'Three wise men' – by Maxwell MacLeod, first published in the *Coracle,* the magazine of the Iona Community, 1993. Coracle: ionacomm@gla.iona.org.uk

'Have mercy on your church' – by Ian M Fraser, from *Wind and Fire,* Margaret and Ian M Fraser, Scottish Churches House. Also in *Salted with Fire: Life-stories, Meditations, Prayers,* St Andrew Press, 1999, ISBN 0715207628. Used by permission of Ian M Fraser.

'God of many names' – by Yvonne Morland, first published in *Coracle*, the magazine of the Iona Community, August 2000. ionacomm@gla.iona.org.uk

Two voices – © Jan Sutch Pickard, first published in *Connect* magazine, Winter 1998.

'Herod and the children' – words © Leith Fisher, music by John L. Bell © 1990, Wild Goose Resource Group, Iona Community, Glasgow G2 3DH, Scotland.

Bowed psaltery moments – first published in *Coracle*, the magazine of the Iona Community. Coracle: ionacomm@gla.iona.org.uk

'Three prayers for Candlemas' – by Ruth Burgess, first published in *Coracle*, the magazine of the Iona Community, February 1998. Coracle: ionacomm@gla.iona.org.uk

'Starmaker God' – by Ruth Burgess, first published in *A Book of Blessings*, Ruth Burgess, Wild Goose Publications, 2001, ISBN 1901557480.

'A flame that cannot be put out' – © Jan Sutch Pickard, first published as 'Candlemas' in *Letting go … and holding on*, Gatherings 3, Jan Sutch Pickard, Oystercatcher Publications, 2004.

INDEX OF AUTHORS

ABOUT THE CONTRIBUTORS

Katie Baker is a Methodist minister near Sunderland and an associate member of the Iona Community.

Irene Barratt was born in 1934 in Oldham. She taught adults with learning difficulties until retirement in 2000, and then studied to be a Methodist local preacher. She is married with two children and two grandsons.

Stuart Barrie was born in Govan, Glasgow. He is a retired engineer

John L Bell – With his colleagues, John has produced collections of original songs, compilations of music from the World Church, and books of worship resources and sermons. He works throughout Europe, North America, Australia and New Zealand for churches of all denominations. In 1999 he was honoured by the Presbyterian Church of Canada and the Royal School of Church Music, which bestowed a Fellowship on him; in 2002, he was awarded an honorary doctorate by the University of Glasgow. He is an occasional broadcaster on BBC radio and television.

Pat Bennett is an associate member of the Iona Community. She has been writing prayers, liturgies, hymns and songs since her first visit to Iona in 1996.

Jan Berry is a minister in the United Reformed Church and a tutor in Practical Theology at Northern College, Manchester (part of the Partnership for Theological Education). She enjoys writing and creating liturgy, and is currently working on a Ph.D on women's rituals of transition.

Ruth Bowen is a Friend of the Iona Community. She divides her time between her home, family and work as a learning support teacher in Clevedon, Somerset, and her island home on Stronsay, Orkney. She loves the islands, woolcraft, gardening and people! She believes in a ministry of prayer, healing and reconciliation.

Anna Briggs – an artist, writer, singer, knitter and clown, born on Tyneside, lived all over, always looking for something new to make and reach people with, especially people who are out of the loop of love and meaning through illness, war, poverty or some other label or event.

Alix Brown is an integrative psychotherapist who works with abused adolescents. She lives with her partner, Polly, and a number of animals in Shropshire. She and Polly are members of the Iona Community.

Nick Burden lives in Newcastle upon Tyne and worships at St Gabriels Heaton Church.

Ruth Burgess is a writer and an editor who lives in the North East of England with a large and hungry black and white cat. She enjoys markets and fireworks and growing flowers and food. She is a member of the Iona Community.

David J. M. Coleman – For too long, Iona Community member David J.M. Coleman gritted his teeth through 'nativity' plays in which donkeys, glitterbugs, robins and snowmen end up with a more prominent role than any remotely biblical characters. He is parent to Taliesin and Melangell, married to Zam, and grateful to the guinea pigs of Barrhead United Reformed Church, who first performed the plays in this book, and with whom he works as minister.

Frances Copsey – 'I continue to struggle with words and MS, and now with the internet too!' More poems by Frances Copsey at www.msplus.pwp.blueyonder.co.uk

Ian Cowie came to the Iona Community on leaving the hospital and army back in 1945. He was the first Iona Abbey guide, then served as a minister in three parishes and finally as chaplain to the Christian Fellowship of Healing. He published five books: *Growing Knowing Jesus, People Praying, Across the Spectrum, Prayer and Ideas for Healing Services* (Wild Goose Publications), and *Jesus' Healing Works and Ours* (Wild Goose Publications), and was a regular contributor to Wild Goose anthologies. Ian died in 2005 at age 81.

da Noust is an informal circle of members and friends of L'Arche Edinburgh. L'Arche is an ecumenical community welcoming adults with learning difficulties, assistants and others to a shared life. The word Noust is Orcadian for a boat shelter on the shore, a place to withdraw for rest and renewal, prior to setting out fishing once more in the morning. For more information about L'Arche please contact L'Arche Edinburgh, 132 Constitution Street, Edinburgh EH6 6AJ. da_noust@yahoo.co.uk

Ed Daub is an associate of the Iona Community, a retired Presbyterian minister (who served the United Church of Christ in Japan, 1951–1963, as a Fraternal Worker), and Professor Emeritus of the University of Wisconsin-Madison, where he initiated the programme in technical Japanese.

John Davies is a member of the Iona Community and a parish priest. He writes online at www.johndavies.org

Lisa Debney lives in Ilkley, West Yorkshire with her husband and four children. She is a member of TranscenDance Co. and works for Barnabas Live (Bible Reading Fellowship).

Carol Dixon was born and brought up in Alnwick, Northumberland and is a lay preacher in the United Reformed Church, recently serving as the National Lay Preaching Commissioner. She works as Moderator's secretary in the Northern Synod Office, is a member of an ecumenical prayer fellowship, the Companions of Brother Lawrence, and is a Friend of St Cuthbert's, Holy Island. She enjoys writing Northumbrian songs, and her hymns have been published in *All Year Round, Songs for the New Millennium, Worship Live* and the new Church of Scotland hymnary. She is married and has a daughter and twin sons.

Leith Fisher has worked as a minister in Glasgow's East end and in Falkirk. He is currently minister at Wellington Church of Scotland, Glasgow. He has been a member of the Iona Community since 1966.

Brian Ford – 'I am aged 58. I teach biology as at a sixth form college. I write and perform poems and songs just for fun.'

Andrew Foster is an engineer living in Ontario, a Friend of the Iona Community, an elder in the Presbyterian Church in Canada, a frequent visitor to Iona, and a contributor to two of Ruth Burgess's previous books, *Friends and Enemies* and *A Book of Blessings*.

David Fox was born in Newbridge, Monmouthshire. He studied chemistry at University College London and taught for a while in Reading. Now a minister of the United Reformed Church serving in Penarth, he has contributed to a number of ecumenical publications for Cytûn and CTBI.

Ian M Fraser – 'The main thing about my life is that Margaret married me, I have three children, nine grandchildren and two great- grandchildren. I became a member of the Iona Community in 1941.'

Kathy Galloway is the current leader of the Iona Community.

Liz Gibson lives in Oban with her husband Martyn and their sons Paul and Hamish. She is a Church of Scotland minister and a hospital chaplain. She brings her experience of theatre and literature to her church's Worship Group. Becoming a member of the Iona Community in 1998, she has been involved with the community's centres on Iona and at Camas on the isle of Mull.

John Harvey is a member of the Iona Community.

Margaret Harvey is a founder member of the Coleg y Groes Community and helps to run Coleg y Groes Retreat House in Corwen, North Wales www.coleggroes.co.uk She is a native of Wales and a Church of Wales priest.

Frances Hawkey is an associate member of the Iona Community who worked for a year as the housekeeper at Iona Abbey. She and her husband, David, now live in Coventry where they are involved in local and world justice issues, and in the work of the International Centre for Reconciliation based at the Coventry Cathedral.

Annie Heppenstall-West was born in Yorkshire, grew up in the Midlands, studied theology at Cambridge, then came back to Yorkshire, where she lives with her husband and son. She is a member of All Hallows Church, Leeds.

Penny Hewlett has a husband, 4 children, a part-time job, an untidy house, and a love of creating resources for the church, especially for young people.

Jim Hughes is a member of the Iona Community. He has spent most of his working life in industry and university teaching.

Isaac Hutchings – Isaac likes the idea that more people will sing his carol and they might teach others so that 'more and more and more (people) will sing their love to Jesus'. Isaac is the youngest of four and loves to try most things except vegetables! His hobbies are rock climbing, Rescue Heroes and digging holes.

Beryl Jeanne is an artist, wordsmith, creative retreat leader and mother, who lives and worships in Birmingham.

Anne Lawson is Vicar of Haslington and Crewe Green in the Chester Diocese.

Pat Livingstone composes music mostly for specific groups. 'O glorious God of the stars' was written for her group Oran and appears on their CD *I Saw a Stranger*. 'On the mountainside' was written for schoolchildren.

Rachel Mann is an Anglican curate in South Manchester. As a poet and liturgist she aims to enable people to encounter the gaps between words where God waits to make herself known. Her perfect day involves watching creaky old films, eating good food and drinking even better wine.

Joy Mead is a well-known writer and the author of *The One Loaf: An everyday celebration*, *A Telling Place: Reflections on stories of women in the Bible*, and *Making Peace in Practice and Poetry*, all published by Wild Goose. She is a member of the Iona Community.

Rosie Miles lives in Birmingham and lectures in English at the University of Wolverhampton. She has contributed to a number of Wild Goose books.

Margaret Moakes – After a varied life as wife, mother, editor, administrator, lay reader and soul friend, Margaret Moakes feels drawn, in widowhood and retirement, to explore more fully the creativity of writing.

Peter Millar is a member of the Iona Community and author of several books, including *Our Hearts Still Sing* (Wild Goose Publications).

Yvonne Morland is a member of the Iona Community.

Carolyn Morris was a teacher in hospitals and primary schools for many years. She is now appreciating life in a new way as an author-craftsperson.

Mary Palmer has an MA in creative writing and has had poems published in many magazines. She also performs her work in a wide range of venues and runs workshops. She contributes to Sanctuary, an alternative worship group.

Alison Pearson is a teacher and writer with an interest and involvement in the use of poetry and story-telling and drama and dance in worship.

Neil Paynter has worked in nursing homes, homeless shelters and homes for people with various challenges. He is now an editor/writer. His books include *Lent & Easter Readings from*

Iona, This is the Day: Readings and Meditations from the Iona Community, Blessed Be Our Table, and *Holy Ground* (with Helen Boothroyd), all published by Wild Goose.

Jan Sutch Pickard is a poet and storyteller, Methodist lay preacher and a member of the Iona Community, based in Mull. For six years she worked on Iona, latterly as Warden of the Abbey. As this publication went to press, she was volunteering on the West Bank with the Ecumenical Accompaniment Programme of the World Council of Churches.

Chris Polhill is a member of the Iona Community and co-author of *Eggs & Ashes: Liturgical and Practical Resources for Lent and Easter* (Wild Goose Publications).

Karen Reeves is a member of the Iona Community.

Jill Rhodes – 'I am an associate member of the Iona Community, and a psychodynamic counsellor, at present living in Belize, Central America, where I work in an Anglican secondary school. Writing and painting are my recreations.'

Richard Sharples is a Methodist minister, and an Iona Community member, currently serving as Warden of Iona Abbey. He is married to Biddy, and father of Annie, Mary and Eve.

Thom M Shuman is a poet and Presbyterian pastor in Cincinnati, Ohio, where he lives with his wife, Bonnie. His son, Teddy, a cancer survivor as well as a person with multiple disabilities, lives nearby. Thom blogs at www.occasionalsighting.blogspot.com

Liz Gregory-Smith lives with her husband in New Brancepeth, near Durham. They have two adult sons. Liz is a Reader at the local Anglican church and works with guests in a creative writing project at St Cuthberts Hospice.

Pat Stubbs – 'As a Friend of the Iona Community, I have been visiting the island since 1959. Before retirement I was an art teacher. For the past 8 years I have taught Sunday school classes at our village church, St Michael's, in Aynho, Northants. I have 3 grown-up children and 5 grandchildren.

Cath Threlfall is married to Peter, with three grown-up sons and one teenage daughter. She works in the care sector helping to support people with severe physcial and learning disabilities.

Marjorie Tolchard – 'I am a retired school librarian. I have two stepsons and a son and a daughter, all grown up and flown the nest. One of my stepsons has a 13-year-old son. The other has a 10-year-old son and a 3-year-old daughter. I live in a very small village in Northamptonshire where I edit the village newsletter and write a local news column for the local weekly paper. My hobbies are gardening, writing and embroidery. I belong to a local history society, a gardening club and two writers' groups.

Rosie Watson lives in Hertfordshire with her husband and a walled garden. She rejoices at the return of the pink bloom to the fields, but thanks God for all she has learnt about him in the long intervening years.

Wellspring was born in 1998 when Catherine McElhinney and Kathryn Turner began making resources, used in parishes and schools, available to the wider world, particularly through their website www.wellsprings.org.uk

Lynda Wright lives in Falkirk, Fife where she has been involved for twelve years in the ministry of hospitality at Key House, a small residential retreat for groups and individuals. This ministry grew out of her three years as Centre Warden at the Abbey on Iona.

THE IONA COMMUNITY IS:

- An ecumenical movement of men and women from different walks of life and different traditions in the Christian church
- Committed to the gospel of Jesus Christ, and to following where that leads, even into the unknown
- Engaged together, and with people of goodwill across the world, in acting, reflecting and praying for justice, peace and the integrity of creation
- Convinced that the inclusive community we seek must be embodied in the community we practise

Together with our staff, we are responsible for:

- Our islands residential centres of Iona Abbey, the MacLeod Centre on Iona, and Camas Adventure Centre on the Ross of Mull

and in Glasgow:

- The administration of the Community
- Our work with young people
- Our publishing house, Wild Goose Publications
- Our association in the revitalising of worship with the Wild Goose Resource Group

The Iona Community was founded in Glasgow in 1938 by George MacLeod, minister, visionary and prophetic witness for peace, in the context of the poverty and despair of the Depression. Its original task of rebuilding the monastic ruins of Iona Abbey became a sign of hopeful rebuilding of community in Scotland and beyond. Today, we are about 250 Members, mostly in Britain, and 1500 Associate Members, with 1400 Friends worldwide. Together and apart, 'we follow the light we have, and pray for more light'.

For information on the Iona Community contact:
The Iona Community, Fourth Floor, Savoy House, 140 Sauchiehall Street,
Glasgow G2 3DH, UK. Phone: 0141 332 6343
e-mail: ionacomm@gla.iona.org.uk; web: www.iona.org.uk

For enquiries about visiting Iona, please contact:
Iona Abbey, Isle of Iona, Argyll PA76 6SN, UK. Phone: 01681 700404
e-mail: ionacomm@iona.org.uk